RECIPES
FOR
SUCCESS

"A cookbook with a recipe for life"

Mark Allen Waltrip

Lee & Kim -
    you Made us Proud to be
Americans, and even prouder
to be your Friends!
              Mark & Karen

First printing, September, 2009.
Second printing, June, 2010.
Third printing, June, 2011

The author can be contacted via email at:
recipesforsuccess.life@gmail.com

To Karen, my wife and best friend,
who met me when I had nothing and gave me
everything of value I have today.

This book would not have been possible without the loving help of my "Sous Chefs". Special thanks to my focus group of Blake, Pamela, Bud, Shaun, and Joe. Your comments were insightful, sometimes painful, but always appreciated. Last, but certainly not least, I want to thank my artistic director, Jon, for pulling this together and adding the finishing touches.

TABLE OF CONTENTS

Foreword by Cara Waltrip

As far back as I can remember our father would tell my brother and me that every parents' dream is that their children live a better life than they did. It was not until I was much older that I learned what that really meant to him. Growing up, our parents were the models of success – great careers, involved in the community, and most of all, wonderful parents. It was not until I was much older that I learned about the many challenges my father had to overcome in his life. Challenges that would have given him every reason to not be the person he ultimately became. He was determined to break the cycle that he grew up in and make sure we lived a much better life than he did. And no matter what challenge we faced in life, he would remind us that if you work hard and do the right things for the right reasons, life would take care of itself.

Even though he achieved success in his professional career, I know that his greatest success is our family. He will also tell you that everything he learned about being a parent he learned from our mother. They saw greatness in my brother and me, even in our most disappointing times, they loved us unconditionally and never let us give up on our dreams. They also supported us in every endeavor and showed us by example how to be a leader, partner, parent and friend.

Both Brian and I followed our dreams, found careers where we get paid doing what we love, and started building our own recipes for success. We have both found partners who bring us so much happiness and are living the lives we always wanted. Most importantly, we have held on to our values and our faith, and continually try to be the best human beings we can be. None of this would have been possible without our parent's love, guidance and support.

For those of you reading this book, you will see the recipes my father followed to write his recipe for success. What he may not realize is that I have been following his recipes my entire life. I know that with a dash of him, a pinch of mom, and splash of brother, I can accomplish anything I want in life.

Your Sous Chef, Cara

WRITING YOUR RECIPE

Life is a lot like cooking. You select your ingredients, mix them together, and create your own dish. Your life is a dish that only you can create and whether or not it turns out the way you planned you are responsible for the results. Life is a lot like cooking because you get to eat what you make.

Any chef knows that a good dish requires choosing the right ingredients and bringing them together with a thoughtful and well-executed plan of action – a recipe! Living a great life requires a great recipe and a great recipe is more than just a list of ingredients and a series of steps to follow. You have to start with a vision of what you want to create, carefully choose the right ingredients, and follow a process that will allow you to create something truly special. Every ingredient must have a purpose and be introduced at the right time and place. If you really think about it, life is a lot like cooking, and the difference between success and failure is the recipe you use.

Using a recipe is really about being consistent in how you approach something. You can make a great meal without a recipe, but the ability to repeat that accomplishment without a recipe requires either tremendous skill or luck. Just remember that recipes are a guideline and should not be written in stone. The real advantage of using a recipe is having the ability to track your progress and make adjustments to improve the outcome. I constantly rewrite my recipes by adding or subtracting ingredients, or changing the timing and temperature until I get it right. I believe the difference between success and failure is the recipe you use and the best recipes are developed over time with plenty of practice, trial and error.

I have also learned that if you don't follow a basic recipe you can lose sight of what is really important. Like most important lessons in life, I learned this one the hard way.

Have you ever had one of those days where you are extremely busy, someone you really care about calls you on your cell phone, and you have to think twice about answering the call? It would be so easy to just send them to voice mail and call them back later.

Don't ever make that mistake. I used to do it all of the time, but one call changed everything.

I was in a meeting when I received a call from my wife, Karen. We had spoken right before the meeting started and agreed to go to lunch as soon as I was done. The meeting was running long when my cell phone rang. I looked down and saw "Karen" on my caller ID. I knew she had arrived a little early and was waiting outside. Karen is the type of person who is always on time. I, on the other hand, made a point of compacting so much into my schedule that someone was always waiting for me. Karen would remind me that I need to be more respectful of other people's time, but I had convinced myself that she just did not understand how much I had on my plate.

When I saw "Karen" on my caller ID, I almost sent her to voice mail. I figured I could wrap the meeting up and call her back as I headed out the door. But for some reason that I cannot explain, I interrupted the meeting and answered the call.

At the other end of the call was Karen crying hysterically. She was in her car, less than two blocks from my office, when she was hit head-on by another driver who had just run through a red light.

The accident happened so close to my office that I arrived at the accident scene just moments before the police and ambulances. Karen's car was completely demolished and she was lying on the curb where she had stumbled from the wreck. We later learned that the combined speed of both vehicles in the accident was over 70 mph and it was nothing short of a miracle that the impact did not kill her instantly.

We rushed her to the hospital where we discovered that her neck was severely damaged. It took over three years and three major surgeries to get her to the point that she could manage the pain.

You will understand more about Karen and the impact this day had on our lives as you read this book. The point I want you to understand and is the most important thing I could ever tell you is that your life can change at any moment. The only thing we really control is how we deal with the challenges that life presents us. This one event completely changed my perspective on life and the people I care about. Just as importantly, it changed my definition of success.

Taking care of Karen during this difficult time also motivated me to get in the kitchen. We could not go out to dinner like we used to, so I had to find something to do that we could enjoy together. We both loved great food and wine, so cooking became my new hobby.

The kitchen became a place where I could relax and focus my attention on something other than life's daily challenges. It is really hard to think about anything else when you are preparing an intricate meal.

Eventually, Karen started getting better and was able to gradually get in the kitchen and cook with me. Our "date night" from our pre-accident life was replaced with "cooking night." We would open a bottle of wine, spread our ingredients out on the table, start chopping, and create new dishes together. One of the many joys of cooking is sharing your creations with others; but the real fun is when you can stand side-by-side with someone you care about and create great dishes together.

Once Karen's health improved, we used every opportunity to travel the world and meet people from all walks of life. What we enjoyed most was the chance to experience different cultures and sample the unique flavors of the foods they create. From the bayous of Louisiana to a small family owned restaurant in Florence, Italy, we have discovered that local cuisines are as rich and varied as the people who live there.

We also found that no matter where you go in the world, food is the centerpiece of how people recognize important milestones in their lives. Rarely do people celebrate anything without good food and friends to share it with. In many ways, good food and success are inexorably linked to the quality of our lives.

These experiences taught us that while there are a great many cultural and social differences that set us apart, there is a basic goodness in people and an inherent desire to be successful. What truly sets us apart is whether we are fortunate enough to be in a place where we can influence the ingredients that make up the recipe of our lives.

Interestingly enough, most people can instantly tell you what their favorite food is, but very few can tell you without hesitation what success really means to them. This is surprising considering the fact that your life is the most important recipe you will ever create.

So how do you create your recipe for success? There are plenty of great self-help and success programs out there, but I believe too many of them tell you how to be successful without asking the most important question of all – "What does success really mean to you in your life?" The purpose of this book is to help you answer this question and encourage you to create your own recipe for success.

It has been my experience that true success is a very personal journey based on very personal criteria. There is no "one-size-fits-all" recipe for achieving success in your life and there is certainly no "poster child" for success whom everyone can strive to emulate. True success is a unique and very personal experience based on your values, goals, and God-given talents.

Unfortunately, too many people define success by the measures of fame, money, power, or possessions, and tend to idolize famous people for the lifestyle these measures have afforded them. Over the years I have had the opportunity to meet and interact with many famous and "successful" people. Unfortunately, I have found that some of these famous and "successful" people are not really successful beyond their fame or financial rewards. Being famous does not always equate to being happy, let alone satisfied with your life. Many of the famous people I have met had to do things to achieve their fame and fortune most people would find impossible to do, like sacrifice their relationships with friends and family. If happiness is one of your goals in life then being famous should not be your litmus test for success.

Take my life for instance. If you met me today, you would

think I am very successful. I have a wonderful family, a respectable profession, and have achieved a great many things in my life; but it was not always this way. As you learn more about my life, you will see that I am truly blessed to be where I am today. I would go so far as to say there were periods in my life when I was far from being someone you would envy.

This does not mean you should not admire successful people. What it does mean is that you need to be very selective as to whom you choose as your role model for success. You need to really think about what success means to you and what drives your personal satisfaction and happiness. There is nothing wrong with shooting for the stars, but as my mother used to tell me, "Be careful what you wish for because you just may get it."

You also have to be careful not to place too much value on fame and material possessions. Look at what happened to our society in the final decades of the 20th century. We became the "bling" generation that always had to have the latest toy. Too many people over-mortgaged their houses, ran up their credit cards, and buried themselves in debt just for a small taste of what it felt like to be "successful."

But then they had to pay the piper. By 2008 the credit markets had frozen, consumer debt skyrocketed, and our very existence as a nation was threatened by financial turmoil. We spent ourselves into a recession and found ourselves standing at the precipice of financial catastrophe that rivaled the Great Depression. We can point fingers at the banks or the government for not intervening, but at the end of the day we only have ourselves to blame. We became too enamored with our lifestyles and allowed greed to drive our ambitions.

However, something very interesting is happening across the country right now. People are starting to embrace the simple things we took so much for granted. Families are staying home and eating together, taking walks in the park, and staying with relatives rather than hotels while they travel. Everywhere I go, people tell me stories of how they are reconnecting with their past and learning to appreciate the simple things in life.

A few years ago during Christmas, our family decided that rather than buy presents for each other we would create something that represents how we feel about each other. We made collages of old pictures, passed down heirlooms to our children and grandchildren, and crafted handmade ornaments for our tree. And you know what? We had the best Christmas we could ever imagine - better than all of those years when we tried to outspend our means to make an impression. We all sat in a circle at the base of the tree, held hands, told stories, laughed, cried, and rekindled our love for each other.

In fact, it was on that day I decided to write this book. It started as a letter to my family to share with them my life story and how the people I have met along the way have shaped and blessed my life. I wanted them to understand that success should never be based on someone else's terms. True success comes from knowing what makes you happy and using this emotion to kindle your passion and achieve your goals, whatever they are. It also means taking personal responsibility for your life and not using the crutches of blame and recrimination to explain your shortcomings.

I call this book "Recipes for Success" because cooking is my passion and some of my best memories in life revolve around cooking and dining with my family and friends. As I look back, most of my successes came as a result of using the mixture of ingredients I picked up along the way. It was not enough just to work hard or get a good education. There are dozens of ingredients that must be brought together in harmony, much like some of my favorite dishes. Everything we do, everyone we meet, and every experience we have develops into the ingredients that create our recipe for life. Life is so much sweeter when it is properly cultivated, prepared, and seasoned to taste.

This book will introduce you to some of my life's experiences, both good and bad, and share with you the ingredients that helped me to achieve my version of success. As I said before, this book is not intended to tell you the specific things you need to do in order to be successful. I am simply sharing my recipe with you in hope that it will encourage you to create your own recipe for success. That is the great thing about cooking for yourself — there is no right or wrong way to do it. You decide on the dish you want to make and you get to pick the ingredients. Just remember, you have to digest what you have created so be very careful of what you place into your dish.

If you don't get it right the first time, change the recipe. One of our greatest gifts in life is the ability to learn from our experiences. You just have to open your mind to the possibility that everything happens for a reason. It is the bad times that help us appreciate the good ones; our losses build the foundation for future wins and our failures show us where we need to improve. Your journey is so much easier to navigate when you realize that past failures represent golden opportunities to learn, progress, and create something new and exciting with your life.

I will let you in on a little secret. The last recipe is my favorite and is called "Balancing the Ingredients." As you will see, I place a great emphasis on finding balance in your life — doing something for yourself that clears your mind and refreshes your soul. As you can probably guess, one of the ways I have found balance in my life is through my cooking. It is very hard to focus on life's trials and tribulations while you are creating a new dish. Throughout this book, I have included many of the recipes I have learned and created over the years. If you don't like this book, at least you will eat well!

Like most recipes, I will start with the ingredients I have used to create my life. Each recipe will introduce certain ingredients to the mixture that has created my version of success. I encourage you to add and delete those ingredients that don't fit your taste. I like spicy food — particularly Italian. You may be a "meat-and-potatoes" person, but that does not mean your dish will be any better or worse than mine. It is your dish; so create it to your taste. ***Bon Appétit!***

GETTING STARTED – THE BASICS

As the cover of this book states, this is a cookbook with a recipe for life. Each chapter that follows represents a chapter of my life and includes the essential ingredient that I learned from these experiences. I have always believed that life is a series of lessons - some good and others not so good. The key is to try and learn something from every experience life gives you. I also believe the day you stop learning is the day you start dying.

I have learned many more lessons in my life than I could ever put in one book, but these are the essential ones that helped me understand and create my definition of success. Just remember that these are my ingredients and, while they have worked for me, it is up to you to select your ingredients based on your goals, values and God-given talents. But here is a little tip to help you select your ingredients – before you start any trip, know where you are going! Sit down and really consider what is important in your life and ask yourself these important questions:

> What are your goals?
> What do you value most?
> What are your talents?

If living a great life is important to you then make sure you understand what "great" really means to you. I have learned that the path from good to great is paved with a mixture of honest critique and self-reflection. You have to start by being honest with yourself and have the courage to be introspective and take responsibility for everything that happens in your life.

This book is also about cooking and each chapter has a recipe that I have created to reflect that chapter of my life. I have included even more of my favorite recipes following the last chapter. I have tried to keep these recipes short, simple and easy to follow, but it does help to have a few basic tools and techniques before you try these recipes. You will notice that most of my recipes follow the same process. I refer to this as the Italian method of cooking.

I enjoy eating and cooking foods from all over the world, but my true love will always be Italian food. There is something about the beauty, simplicity, and flavor of Italian food that has captured my heart. When we visit Italy, we always try to find those little family-owned restaurants the locals prefer. I will never forget a little family owned restaurant called Ristorante Miky that we found on the beach in Monterosso. Monterosso is the northern-most village of the Cinque Terre region on the coast of Tuscany. We stopped there for lunch one day and had the most magnificent meal you could ever imagine. Not only was the food fantastic, but also the presentation rivaled any 5-star restaurant we had ever been to.

When the meal was over, I went back to the kitchen and asked to speak to the chef so I could thank him for the wonderful meal he had prepared for us. Unfortunately, he did not speak English and my Italian was no better. But afterwards, the waitress brought him to our table and introduced him to us. It turns out the chef was her father Miky and their family had owned and operated restaurants in the area for several generations. I would have bet lunch that the chef who prepared our meal was classically trained at one of the great European culinary institutes, but the fact is, everything he knew about cooking he learned from his father, who learned from his father, and so on and so on.

That is why I love Italian food. Not just for the food, but also for the passion and love for their food they have handed down from generation to generation. It takes great passion to create great food. As we traveled around Italy, I would always find my way back to the kitchen to sneak a few moments with the chef and thank them for the dishes they created for us. Most chefs toil away in the kitchen without much notice from their guests and they are absolutely delighted when you take the time to thank them. It is also where I had some of my best cooking lessons. Great chefs have a passion for their craft and people with passion make the best teachers.

It was in these kitchens I learned what I refer to as the "Italian method" of cooking. This method is based on three simple concepts: 1) always use fresh ingredients; 2) cook them in the proper order; and, 3) cook them for the right amount of time. As you go through my recipes you will notice they all have a similar pattern of fresh ingredients, order, and timing. Every ingredient has a specific consistency and flavor that is determined by how it is introduced to the dish. For instance, fresh onions by themselves can be very bitter, but sauté them in oil for 3-5 minutes and they start to create a more pleasant flavor as the natural sugars are released. Sauté them on a medium flame for 20-25 minutes more and they will caramelize into a thick and sweet flavor.

You will notice I apply this method to all of my recipes, including Asian, French, Spanish, and American dishes. I have also included recipes for most of the sauces, rubs, and mixes that are used in these dishes, such as ketchup, taco seasoning, and Creole seasoning. While you can substitute prepackaged mixes in any of these recipes, you will find that most items that come off the shelves of a store have too much sodium and not enough flavor. That is why I prefer to mix everything from scratch. Besides, most of these mixes store very well, so you can make a large batch for later use. For instance, when I make my BBQ sauce, I make enough to last several months. Just remember to label your mixes and use a vacuum sealer when freezing items for longer-term storage.

I typically do not make very complicated dishes that require a lot of ingredients. Some of the best dishes I have created use only a few ingredients. Some of my favorite dishes use what chefs refer to as the "holy trinity" of ingredients — onions, celery, and carrots. Cooked together in the proper order and timing, these ingredients can produce a fantastic flavor profile.

Always remember that cooking should be fun and the fun part about cooking is being creative and trying new things. So make sure you take the liberty to deviate from these recipes and make them your own. For instance, I love the flavor of hot cherry peppers. I use them in everything from Bolognese sauce to gumbo. You may prefer a different flavor profile, so be sure to try and mix a few ingredients of your own to each dish. Remember, there is no right or wrong way to make these dishes. All that matters is you get to enjoy the dish you create with the people you love and care about.

Basic Techniques:

Probably the most daunting aspect of cooking for most people is learning basic techniques. I am a Food Network junkie and try to watch as many shows as possible to expand my knowledge base. Unfortunately, most of what you see on TV cooking shows is designed to impress and entertain rather than to teach. There are a few shows I would highly recommend for both beginner and accomplished cooks because they know how to make food fun, and you can actually gain practical knowledge just from watching them. These include Giada De Laurentiis's "Every Day Italian," and Bobby Flay's "Throwdown." I like Giada because she blends her rich Italian heritage with solid culinary training to create great dishes most people can replicate in their own kitchen. She makes cooking an entertaining experience that can be achieved by the average person. Bobby also makes cooking a lot of fun, but I really like the intense flavor profiles he creates. He will definitely stimulate your imagination by introducing combinations of ingredients you would not normally consider.

I have tried to keep my recipes very simple and easy to read. There are several techniques referenced in these recipes designed to create the right texture and flavor for each dish. The key thing to remember is that food can be very forgiving, so it is not necessary to measure or chop everything perfectly. It is more important to use fresh ingredients in the proper order for the right amount of time. Here are some basic terms and techniques that will help you with these recipes:

Sliced: As the name implies, this is simply cutting the

ingredient in thin slices across its natural side. Slicing allows a release of flavor, while maintaining the shape and texture of the ingredient.

Chopped: This involves cutting your ingredient in small squares the size of your finger tip. This usually results in a rougher texture for the dish.

Diced: This involves cutting your ingredient in small squares, ¼ the size of a chopped ingredient. This usually results in a slightly smoother texture for the dish.

Minced: This involves cutting your ingredient in very small pieces that are almost the size of a peppercorn. You can use your miniature food processor to create this condition.

Caramelized: This is a chemical process that uses heat to release sugar and caramel flavors in an ingredient, particularly onions. The key is to not allow the onions to burn, so you must stir them constantly. In a hot pan, add olive oil and continually toss the onion slices for up to 30 minutes until they reach a dark, rich brown color. The brown color is the sugar in the onion caramelizing.

Sauté: This is a method of cooking ingredients in a pan with oil over high heat. Sauté comes from the French word "Sauter" which means "to jump" and refers to the method of flipping food in the air as more accomplished chefs do when they sauté a dish. The key to properly sautéing a dish is to stir it constantly until it is fully cooked. Also, make sure you use oil suitable for use with high heat such as olive oil or clarified butter. Regular butter may taste great, but it will burn under higher temperatures. In addition, I would not waste money using extra virgin olive oil to sauté under high heat. Extra virgin olive oil is produced from the first pressing of olives and is the most pure and the best tasting olive oil. But like most fine oils, it will break down under heat. Pure olive oil is cheaper and works just fine for this use. Save your extra virgin olive oil for salad dressings and garnishes.

Braised: Braising is a combination cooking method typically used for meats where the food is first seared at a high temperature and then finished in a covered pot with a liquid. The key step to braising is to sear the meat at high heat to lock in its natural juices and flavors. The next step is to slow cook the meat in a liquid mixture that provides enough moisture to break down any tough connective tissues. When braising meat, I always hand rub the meat with spices and allow it to rest at room temperature for at least one hour. In order to further seal in the flavors, lightly dust the meat with finely sifted flour. Make sure the pan is pre-heated and use good oil suitable for high heats. Most meat can be browned to a nice golden brown with 2-3 minutes on each side.

Reduced: This is the process of using heat to evaporate some of the liquid from a dish. In most of my recipes, I will reduce wine or stock to create a thicker consistency and more intense flavor. Always remember that reducing the liquids in a dish does not reduce the other ingredients. That is why I always recommend using low-sodium chicken broth so you do not end up with an overly salty dish. You also have to be careful when using other salty foods, such as pancetta, that may infuse too much salt when liquids are reduced.

Deglazing (scraping): Some of the best flavors in your dish will come from the caramelized meat or vegetables that get stuck to the bottom of a pan after braising or sautéing. Deglazing is the process of introducing a liquid to the already-hot pan and scraping free these tidbits from the bottom of the pan. I typically use wine for deglazing, but you can also use any type of meat or vegetable stock. Once the liquid is introduced, use your spatula to scrape the bottom and mix it into the other ingredients.

Pre-heating the pan: The secret to properly braising or sautéing an ingredient is to get the pan to the proper temperature before introducing the oil. Most of my recipes call for pre-heating the pan. Simply set the pan on the open flame or burner and adjust the heat to the specified temperature. Let it sit there for 3-5 minutes until you can feel the heat radiating from the pan. Do not touch the pan! Then add the oil and use your spatula to disperse evenly across the bottom of the pan. Always test the heat by dropping one small piece of the ingredient, to gauge the reaction of the oil. When the oil is ready, it will instantly bubble up around the edges of the ingredient.

Some kitchen tools you will need:

There are a lot of tools you will need to have fun in the kitchen. This is not intended to be a complete list, but it will give you some ideas on some of the more important items you should have on hand:

Good set of knives: You are more likely to cut yourself using dull or cheap knives. Make sure you find a set of knives that are comfortable to hold and well balanced. I believe you are better off having two or three really good knives, instead of a cheap set. The most used knife is an 8" to 10" chef knife. You will also need a smaller paring knife.

A good set of pots and pans: Good pans with a heavy bottom are a must for anyone who really likes to cook. You want to find something that can evenly displace the heat. While non-stick pans are easy to clean, they are not good for braising and sautéing, especially if you want to capture the intense flavor of deglazing the pan. My favorite pan is a very large

15" pan that I use to braise meat. I would also pick up a black iron skillet. They are not very expensive, but make sure you properly cure your black iron skillet before using. To cure your black iron skillet, make sure you first wash it thoroughly to remove any existing coatings from the manufacturer. Then grease the skillet on the inside thoroughly with a light coat of vegetable oil and bake it in your oven at 350 degrees for at least one hour. You will also want a good "Dutch" oven, which is a very heavy pot with a lid that you can use in the oven or on the stove top.

Miniature food processor: Most people have a large food processor and rarely use them. A small food processor (typically 2-4 cups), on the other hand, will save you a lot of time in preparing your dishes. For instance, any recipe that calls for a minced vegetable or spice is an ideal candidate for the miniature food processor.

Hand blender (emulsion blender): This is another handy device that will save you a lot of time and make your dishes much better. It will usually save you from having to transfer your dish in stages to a blender or large food processor to create cream sauces and soups. Always remember to use caution when blending hot liquids.

Oil thermometer: The secret to any fried food is oil temperature. If it gets too cool, it will emulsify the food with grease. If it gets too hot, it will destroy the flavor. An oil thermometer is a good investment.

Food brushes: I have a variety of brushes that I use for everything from applying BBQ sauce to ribs to coating bruschetta with olive oil. The best brushes have a soft and synthetic bristle that almost resembles little rubber strings.

You may notice that the ingredients listed in my recipes are not organized in the order that they are used. I write and store most of my recipes on my smart phone, and I cut and paste them into my shopping list before I go to the grocery store. Therefore, my ingredients are typically listed in the order that I shop for them, rather than how I use them in my recipes. I also find it much more efficient to cut and prep all of the ingredients before I start cooking.

So now we are ready to get started. You may want to grab a pen and notepad so you can start writing your own recipe. This is my recipe and I hope you enjoy it. ***Bon Appétit!***

RECIPE #1:

COOKING ON THE SIDE OF THE ROAD

The Essential Ingredient:
Accept responsibility for your life

I can remember the first time I knew we were poor. I was 15 years old in the summer of 1975 and we were parked at a roadside rest stop along a highway in Nebraska. My mother was cooking our lunch on the tailgate of our station wagon when a huge recreational vehicle pulled up and parked right next to us. I remember staring in awe at the sheer magnitude of this beautiful "land yacht" as two young girls who were about my age stepped out with their small puppy on a leash. They looked like they had just come out of a beauty salon with their perfect hair and freshly pressed clothes. I was so fixated on them, I did not realize they were staring right back at me; they started to giggle. This was not a flirtatious or friendly giggle for they were clearly laughing at me. At this point, I looked down and realized what they thought was so funny. We had been traveling for weeks, living in tents, and had not bathed in days. I was still wearing the clothes I slept in the night before. We were a pretty rag-tag bunch and we probably looked like vagabonds, traveling around the country looking for work. As I turned away from them in shame, I looked up and realized my mother was standing there watching me the whole time.

"I bet you wish that was you," she said.

I had to admit she was right.

My parents never had much money. They raised us in a small apartment in a neighborhood that divided the inner-city ghettos from the wealthy neighborhoods of Cleveland, Ohio. I could walk a few blocks in one direction and be standing in one of the roughest areas in the city, yet a few blocks in the other direction were some of the largest and most luxurious homes in America. I had friends in both directions and no matter how often my mother would tell me that "money can't buy you happiness," being rich sure looked a lot more fun than being poor.

While we were better off than some of my friends, we were much closer to being poor than wealthy. My father was a high school teacher who never had any financial discipline and always spent what he made and then some. It seemed like we were always going from one financial crisis to another. I remember, as a child, walking home from school one day and finding a $5 bill lying on the sidewalk. I was so excited to rush home and show my mother my newfound treasure, but when I got home, I found my mother sitting on the couch crying. As it turned out, payday was still two days away and we did not have enough money to buy formula for my newborn sister. That $5 saved the day.

I don't think my father actually enjoyed being a teacher, but he liked having his summers off to travel. For as long as I can remember, every summer we would pack up our apartment, put everything in storage, load up the station wagon, and hit the road. We traveled across the country, sleeping in tents and living in campgrounds. By the time I was 15, I had visited every state in the continental United States and hiked and canoed through the backcountry of every major national park.

My parents were avid naturalists who taught us how to live off the land. During these summer trips, we hunted and fished for most of our meals and harvested wild fruits and vegetables from the forests. My mother's favorite book was Stalking the Wild Asparagus by Euell Gibbons. This was the comprehensive guidebook for foraging for food in the wild. When we had to buy food, it was usually beans and rice, so we were pretty motivated to catch fish or hunt for small game. I never remember drinking real milk until I was an adult, but we had plenty of powdered milk on hand. My mother was a wizard with powdered milk; she could even make ice cream with fresh snow, powdered milk, and sugar.

Although we did not have much money, in many ways our life was rich with experiences that most people could only dream of. Unfortunately, our family life also had its dark secrets that impacted us in ways most people would find hard to imagine. You see, the ability to manage finances was not the only discipline my father lacked.

My father was very abusive, had a terrible temper, and it did not take much to set him off. It usually would start with an argument with my mother that would escalate into physical abuse. My older brother James and I would lie on our beds listening to him beat our mother, and knew that when he was done with her, we would be next. When our father burst into the room, he would grab James and start beating him almost mercilessly. Sometimes he would use his hands, but mostly he preferred a belt or strap.

James was very stubborn. When our father took to beating him, he would stiffen up and refuse to cry. This only made our father angrier and the beatings worse. I learned at a very early age to cry as soon as my father turned to me. All he really wanted was to satisfy his obsession for control over someone weaker than himself and, once he extracted the desired reaction, he would stop.

James was one year older than me and the fourth generation of first-born boys named after their father. Our grandfather was a small-town preacher who lived by the saying "Spare the rod and spoil the child." As I discovered later in life, like most child abusers, my father was severely abused by his father when he was a child. To this day, I consider one of my greatest accomplishments leaving that legacy behind.

My mother was a wonderful and loving person, but she lacked the self-confidence to stand up for herself and my father made a point of removing what little confidence she had left. She was the oldest of 12 children that grew up on a farm. She met and married my father when she was 18 and he was 30. I think she saw him as a way to escape the daily chores of taking care of her younger brothers and sisters. I think he saw in her someone whom he could control. Although she could not protect us from him, she was always there for us. She cooked all of our meals and made most of our clothes by hand. By the time I was 10, I started getting teased at school for wearing hand-made clothes. I immediately went and found a series of odd jobs — such as sweeping sidewalks for local shops for 25 cents per store — so I could buy my own clothes. I worked almost every day and I never had to wear hand-made clothes again.

As the years passed, my mother started drinking and, by the time I was a teenager, she had become an alcoholic. Back then we didn't have 12-step programs. Alcoholism was the secret disease no one wanted to talk about. Unfortunately, the more she drank, the more "courageous" she became towards my father. He would come home from work, find her drunk, an argument would start along with the beatings. This was the vicious and dysfunctional cycle we lived in.

Yet on a summer day in 1975, along a Nebraska highway, my life began to change.

I was less than two years from graduating high school and, while most of my friends were trying to decide what college they wanted to attend, I had no delusions that my parents could ever afford such a luxury. I knew I had to escape the path I was on, but I did not have the courage or resources to take that first step. When those two young girls stepped out of their rolling vacation home and pretty much laughed at me, I admit that for a moment I was ashamed and I started to get angry. But then something completely different happened. My anger turned into inner reflection and my reflection turned into resolve. At that particular moment in my life, I decided that one day I would be successful. I also remember saying to myself that one day I would have my own family and that I would never be like my father.

I learned a very important lesson that day — you can't blame others for your place in life. Your life is what you want it to be.

My mother always told me I could do anything I wanted to do; I just had to figure out what I wanted and go for it. It sounds simple enough, but even she never found a way to achieve true success in her life. As I look back on her life, I realize the first step is to take control of your life. This means that from this point forward, you must decide what you want your life to become. You cannot go through life using excuses for not achieving your dreams.

But in order to have control over your life, you must be willing to take responsibility for your actions and accept yourself for who you really are. For most people, this is the most difficult thing to do. It is too easy to blame others for your situation in life.

Blaming others is a weakness that will never allow you to reach your full potential. On the other hand, accepting responsibility means looking introspectively at yourself, owning up to your role in all things that happen in your life, and using each challenge as an opportunity to learn how to be a better person.

When it comes to personal responsibility, I have found that people tend to fall into one of two categories - those who deflect responsibility and those who accept responsibility. Unfortunately, you will find that the majority of people gravitate toward the former category. People that "deflect" responsibility are the ones who use life's challenges as a crutch. You hear them say, "I could have been 'this,' or I could have achieved 'that,' if only I did not have this obstacle in my way." They have taken themselves off the hook for any perceived failure in their life and assigned the responsibility to someone or something else.

Too many people in this world have perfected the art of deflection. Deflection comes in all shapes and sizes. You can blame your parents for how they raised you, your boss for that promotion that never came, or use many other countless explanations for why things did not turn out the way you wanted them to. Guess what? There will be many instances when you were right! There will be instances when you were the victim and the situation was beyond your control. But being right should not be used as an excuse for preventing you from learning from each of these experiences. There will also be instances, if you really look at things objectively, where you may find you could have handled things better, even when you were right.

Another form of deflection is saying, "Bad things happen to

good people." This is nonsense. Bad things can happen to anyone. It's what you do with the various experiences in your life, both good and bad, that determines who you are. I grew up in a very difficult environment with very little opportunity, but that is not what defined me. What defined me was the ability to learn from my experiences, to accept responsibility for my actions, and to work each day at being a better person.

Always remember that no one skates through life without adversity. If you live in a difficult environment or have experienced serious emotional or physical trauma, you are not alone. The only thing that truly sets you apart from others is how you respond to life's challenges. If you gain anything from this book, I would hope it would be this: Don't allow your life to be defined by the bad things that happen along the way and don't be afraid to ask for help[1]. As you will realize later in this book, behind every successful person is a long line of "angels" who helped him or her along the way.

That is why it is so important to look at each thing that happens in your life and ask yourself what you can learn from this so you can be a better person. By looking introspectively at yourself, you will gain something positive from everything that happens in your life, both good and bad. It will also open the door for you to break the negative cycles that may have infiltrated your life.

It took me many years to realize that success in life is not a birthright; it is a privilege that must be earned. While some people may be blessed with certain advantages in life, we all have the opportunity to create our own recipe for success. It also took me many years to realize that growing up, we were never really poor. While money may influence the quality of your standard of living, it does not dictate the quality of your life. Money is something you can earn, but a great life can only be measured in ways that only you can appreciate and understand. You must figure out what is important to you and build your life around that. It all starts with taking responsibility for your life and using every opportunity to learn from life's experiences.

---

[1] See Appendix "A" for a list of helpful resources.

Blackened Tilapia with Creole Sauce

I was born in southern Louisiana in the heart of Cajun Country. Although my parents moved us to Cleveland, Ohio at an early age, we visited the area regularly and my mother raised us on Creole-style food. This particular dish is a fusion of Cajun-style and Creole foods. While the ingredients in Cajun and Creole dishes are similar, there are distinct differences between the two. The word Creole has many meanings, but its cuisine is a cultural mix of West-European, African, Caribbean and native Indian flavors. For the most part, the Creoles represent a blend of Spanish, American, African, German, and Italian people who settled in Southern Louisiana. The Cajuns, on the other hand, are descendants of the French-speaking Acadians who were banished from Nova Scotia in the early 1700s. They settled in southwest Louisiana and lived in the difficult terrain of swamps and bayous. They had to fight to survive and the Cajun farmers, fishermen, and hunters learned how to live off this exotic land. That necessity inspired Cajun cooking, which can make a great meal out of whatever they forged from the swamps.

If I had to make a distinction between Creole and Cajun food, I would simply say this - Creole is a cuisine inspired by a variety of cultural influences, and Cajun is a style of cooking forged by a certain way of life. We ate a lot of Creole-style food growing up, but we lived a Cajun-style of life.

Chef Paul Prudhomme, of K-Paul's Restaurant in New Orleans is widely credited for making Cajun-style cooking popular in America. The first time we ate there was in 1980 when I took my family there to announce my engagement to Karen. His signature dish was Blackened Redfish, for which he created a technique for cooking fish by coating it with clarified butter and sprinkling it with Creole seasoning before searing it in an iron skillet over extremely high heat. This process creates a blackened crust and preserves the natural juiciness of the fish. Since then, Chef Prudhomme's Blackened Redfish has become synonymous with Cajun-style cooking; however, most Cajuns will tell you that they would never purposely burn a perfectly good piece of fish.

This particular dish integrates Chef Prudhomme's Blackened Cajun cooking method with a traditional Creole sauce, just like my mother used to make. Tilapia is the perfect fish for blackening because it is very flavorful and holds together over high heat. You can also substitute red snapper, grouper, or any other "white" fish.

Ingredients for the blackened tilapia:

6 tilapia filets
3 tablespoons blackened rub (see my recipe at the end of the book)
3 cups Creole sauce (see recipe below)
2 cups cooked white rice
2 tablespoons minced green onions
Olive oil
¼ lb butter (1 stick)

Directions for the blackened tilapia:

Using a brush, lightly coat fish filets on each side with the olive oil; dust thoroughly with the blackening rub mix. Set out at room temperature for 15 minutes, turning once.

Note: It is recommended to cook blackened fish outside because of the amount of smoke that is generated.

Heat a cast iron skillet until it's nearly red hot. Drop one-half of the stick of butter into the pan. As soon as the butter starts to turn brown, immediately place the filets in the skillet and cook for 2 minutes per side. Add additional butter after turning, if needed.

You can usually cook 2 or 3 filets at a time. Add more butter and allow the butter to turn brown once more before placing the *additional filets in the skillet.*

Serve with rice and ladle a generous amount of Creole sauce on the rice and fish. Garnish with green onions.

Ingredients for the Creole Sauce:
1 medium onion, chopped
1 green bell pepper, chopped
2 celery ribs, chopped
5 garlic cloves, diced
3 shallots, chopped
2 teaspoons Creole seasoning mix (see recipe)
1 teaspoon hot paprika
1/8 teaspoon cayenne pepper
4 imported bay leaves
1 ¼ cups chicken stock or canned broth
4 medium tomatoes, peeled, seeded, and diced
1 tablespoon Worcestershire sauce
1 teaspoon hot sauce
2 tablespoons unsalted butter
½ teaspoon salt

Directions for the Creole Sauce:
In a large pan or cast iron skillet on medium to high heat, melt butter and then add the onions, bell pepper, and celery. Sauté until vegetables are softened (about 3-5 minutes). Add garlic and shallots and cook for an additional 3 minutes.

Add the Creole seafood seasoning, paprika, cayenne pepper, bay leaves, and chicken stock. Bring to a boil and cook until slightly reduced and thickened, about 5 minutes.

Stir in the tomatoes and cook for 10 minutes longer until thick. Stir in the Worcestershire sauce, hot sauce, salt, and reduce the heat to low. Simmer for 10 minutes. Serve over rice with seafood.

RECIPE #2:

MAKING THE ROUX

The Essential Ingredient:
Work hard

Without a doubt, the most difficult step in any journey is to take the first step. I knew that if I was going to take control of my life, I had to escape my current environment. I had no idea where to go, let alone how to get there. In retrospect, I realize most people fail to achieve their goals simply because of fear —fear of the unknown, fear of failure, and even fear of disappointing their loved ones. I have even seen people like my mother stay in an abusive relationship simply because she was scared she could not make it on her own. Just think of the irony of her situation — she feared being on her own more than the constant abuse she endured.

I believe the only way to overcome fear is with faith. I was very fortunate to have someone in my life at a very early age who was able to teach me the power of faith and to help me understand there will be things in our lives we simply do not comprehend, but have the ability to take us to places we could never imagine.

Whether you are a religious person or not, it is difficult to deny that there is a basic goodness in humankind as well as a universal force that connects all living things. If you have ever stood on the top of a mountain looking out over the forest-covered valleys below, watched the waves of the ocean beat rhythmically along a rocky shore, or watched the sun rise or set on the horizon, you know that special feeling that comes from interacting with the universe around you. Now try to imagine those same scenes in the absence of anything living. If you really think about it, there is not much beauty in the universe without the interaction of the living. You can't always see it, but in your heart, you know it is there. That feeling is the essence of faith.

We can draw on our faith from many sources — our religion, family, and friends — but at some point you have to simply believe in yourself. You must take the first step. Decide what you want your life to be and start heading in that direction.

I doubt there could have ever been a plan conceived that could mirror the roundabout path that led me to where I am today. It took me a long time to understand that the best plans are the plans you never make, and success in life is much more about the journey than the destination.

I am living proof you can accomplish almost anything you want in your life. It does not matter where you come from, whom you know, or what your station in life happens to be. You simply have to develop some very basic principles by which you live your life. I escaped a difficult childhood and bounced around from job to job looking for my path to success, but along the way I met some wonderful people, did some very interesting things, and managed to learn some things that helped me fulfill almost all of my dreams.

I was born in southern Louisiana in a region that shows up as a body of water on most maps. Although we moved to Ohio when I was young, we went back to Louisiana at least once a year; the Cajun culture there greatly influenced my life. Most of my relatives either worked in the oil fields or worked in businesses that in some way relied on the oil industry for their business. When we all got together, it usually involved a bag full of boiled crawfish, a keg of beer, and a big pot of gumbo.

Gumbo is a Louisiana soup that brings together the rich cuisines of regional Indian, French, Spanish, and African cultures. The word "gumbo" is derived from the African term for okra, "gombo." There are no hard-and-fast rules for making gumbo beyond a basic roux, okra, and your imagination. There are probably as many distinctive recipes for gumbo as there are cooks in Louisiana. If you really think about it, gumbo is much like life in general. But what really sets gumbo apart from any other soup is the roux. A roux is a basic mixture of fat and flour that is used as the basis for the entire meal, and it has to be cooked just right to get the proper flavor and consistency. I know chefs who spend hours tending over their roux just to get the right flavor and consistency. It is not uncommon for them to throw it out and start all over again until they get it right. If you think of your life as one big pot of gumbo, the roux is the foundation on which you build your life. Sometimes you have to throw it out and start over many times before you get it right.

I don't know where you are at this moment in your life, but if you ever feel life is hopeless, I want you to know that the greatest gift we have is the ability to make things better. Your mind and body may have their limits, but your heart and soul is an endless resource that can propel you through insurmountable challenges. The key is to never give up until you get it right.

I was barely 17 years old when I graduated high school. A week later, with $50 in my pocket, I left home for good. My only plan was to get an education and make a success of my life. I had no idea how this was going to happen. I grabbed my guitar, a back pack and sleeping bag, and traveled across the country looking for work in the oil fields of Oklahoma, Texas, and Louisiana.

I quickly found work in Oklahoma, but it was without a doubt the worst working conditions I have ever experienced. A few weeks later, someone told me about a job on an offshore rig in the Gulf of Mexico, so I hitchhiked to Port Bolivar, Texas where I signed on with an offshore oil company.

My very first day on the job, we took a crew boat out to one of the rigs. Most of the crew boats were converted Navy PT boats from World War II. They had a deep-V hull that allowed them to cut through 8 to 10-foot waves in the Gulf of Mexico. On that day, we encountered very rough seas and I started to get a little seasick, so I decided to go up top to get some fresh air. While standing on the deck, the boat hit a huge wave that pitched me up and over the side of the boat. Flying through the air, I reached out and grabbed the side rail as I went over. I was holding on for dear life, hanging on to the rail as the waves pounded me against the side of the boat. Just as I was about to lose my grip, a very large wave scooped me up and slammed me back down on the deck. I laid there for about five minutes, my heart pounding through my chest, as I realized we were 20 miles off shore in heavy seas and no one was above deck but me. Had I not been able to hold on, I would have never been found.

There have been several times in my life when I knew I was in danger of being hurt or killed, but this is the one time I was in a situation with no chance of survival. If it were not for the grace of God, I would have never been able to pull myself back into that boat. Interestingly enough, I have never been scared of dying because it is one of the few things in life certain to happen, so I simply accept it. Instead, it is the process of dying that scares me. I am certain there is a God, however, and he has intervened many times throughout my life.

Offshore oilrigs are a rough and dangerous place, and it did not take me long to realize I was not cut out for this type of work. After a few weeks, I decided to hitchhike to Louisiana and look for work in the shipyards outside of New Iberia.

By now, I had pretty much hit rock bottom. I was flat broke and everything I owned was in my backpack. I finally found work at a local day-labor company that supplied temporary labor to the oil fields.

Most of us have seen this image in either movies or on TV — a group of day laborers standing on a corner as a pickup truck pulls up. The boss man gets out and selects one person at a time until he meets his quota for the jobs at hand. The lucky ones get to work some lousy job most people would never even consider. The unlucky ones go home and try again the next day. There was a period in my life when that person was me.

Every morning I showed up at a warehouse at 5 a.m. with about 100 other guys. The local oil companies showed up with a pickup truck and chose a handful of laborers, loaded us in a truck and hauled us to a worksite. You cannot imagine the anticipation, let alone the fear, of not being picked. I was one of the lucky ones — young, in good shape, and no family to take care of.

I will never forget my first day on the job. I was picked up and taken to a warehouse on the other side of town. The warehouse was stacked high with pallets full of 200-pound bags of sand. Parked in the center of the warehouse was a large, empty flatbed trailer. The boss told me to load the flatbed, so I spent the next 30 minutes walking around the warehouse looking for a forklift. About that time, the boss came back and started yelling at me for not starting the job. When I asked him where the forklift was, he looked at me like I was stupid and said, "If the forklift wasn't broke, I wouldn't need your ass to load the truck."

I spent the next 12 hours loading that flat bed one bag at a time. Day labor in the oil fields is backbreaking work. One day we would be out in the shipyards and the next day we would be on some inland rig. But the harder you worked, the better chance you had of getting hired for a permanent position; therefore, each day became a challenge to improve your position.

The work was extremely dangerous. Not a week went by that I didn't see someone get severely injured, and someone actually got killed on one of the jobs. He fell off a 180-foot oilrig we were on. We thought he was lucky because he missed the barge and hit the water feet first. Unfortunately, the force of the fall buried him in the muddy bottom of the bayou, and by the time they found him he was dead.

No matter how bad it got, I never gave up. Little-by-little, day-by-day, I started to develop a reputation as someone who showed up on time, worked hard, and never complained. I would take on any dirty or difficult job and do it to the best of my ability. After a few months, my hard work caught the eye of a small painting and sandblasting contractor named Gerald Waguespack. Gerald hired me on his crew and we spent the next year traveling throughout the Atchafalaya Swamp of southern Louisiana working in shipyards and repairing inland oilrigs.

Gerald was one of the first positive male role models in my life. He was a humble man who had built a small, but respectable business with his bare hands. And it did not take long to find out that he was much smarter than he let on. He taught me the importance of taking pride in my work. His handshake was his bond and he always did what he said he would do.

Although the work was hard, I really enjoyed working for Gerald. Every day was an adventure that took us through the backwoods and swamps along the southern Louisiana coast. We would meet at the shop around 6 a.m., load up the truck with bags of sand and cans of paint, and drive our rig out to various job sites spread around the oil fields. One day we would work on large boats in a shipyard; the next day we would work at an inland oilrig in the middle of nowhere.

The work was also sometimes dangerous. By now, I had lost count of the number of times I saw a serious accident that resulted in either someone getting injured or major property damage. Some of the crane operators in the shipyards would keep a cooler full of beer under their seat and would be three sheets to the wind before the end of their shift. I watched a crane operator drop a two-ton generator on a car as he lifted it off a flatbed in the parking lot. I also saw a crane operator lift a 40-foot I-beam and spin it around so fast it went out of control and cut a portable toilet in half. Thank goodness no one was using it at the time!

The best part of working for Gerald was some of the strange places and interesting people we got to see. It also seemed like Gerald had a relative in every little town in which we stopped. One day we stopped for lunch at a small shack out in the middle of nowhere. Gerald took me inside and introduced me to his "aunt." She was a small, wiry old woman who looked like she was 100 years old. She was standing in front of her stove, stirring a big pot of gumbo. As I looked into the pot, I saw what appeared to be frayed tennis balls bobbing up and down in the gumbo. I asked her what kind of gumbo she was making and she curtly replied in a deep Cajun accent, "I'm making squirrel gumbo." I then asked what the round balls were in the pot and she replied, "We don't waste no part of the squirrel around here. Dem are squirrel heads."

Most people would have probably refused the offer of squirrel head gumbo and, quite frankly, the thought of doing so passed through my mind. But I was hungry and I had eaten squirrel many times before, just never in a gumbo. The truth is it tasted pretty good.

Not too long after that experience I got the call that my cousin, Randy, had fallen off the top of an oilrig, killing him instantly. I knew it was time for a change.

Looking back, I realize this was an important period in my life. I had left home at 17 and managed to survive on my own in some very strange and interesting places. I had also added a very important ingredient to the recipe of my life — you can overcome many of life's challenges with a solid work ethic.

Throughout my life, I have met many people who did just enough to get by. I discovered early on that the harder you work, the more likely people will respect you. When you take the extra effort to make the job better, you will be recognized as a craftsman — someone who brings skill and effort to the job. Eventually you will catch the eye of someone like Gerald who will help change your life.

A good work ethic can also overcome many perceived deficiencies. Rarely is the winner's circle of life filled with the smartest, fastest or strongest person in the arena. It is more often filled by those who have put forth the greatest effort and determination to succeed. The mindset of a true champion is to work harder than anyone else and to never give up. When I left the oil fields and eventually went to college, I managed to complete four college degrees, finish at the top of my class, and completed my Masters and Bachelors degrees in Aerospace Engineering on the same day. I cannot say I was the smartest person in my school, but I am certain that no one in my class worked harder for their grades than I did.

It is also very important to remember just how lucky we are to be living in a place where opportunity exists. In fact, it is too easy to take for granted how good life really is. Sometimes you have to remind yourself that as long as you have your mind and body there is always opportunity.

I recently saw a YouTube video about a young man named Nick

Vujicic[2] that really proves this point. Nick was born without arms or legs due to a rare disorder, yet he travels around the world speaking to groups of young people. He starts out entertaining them with his unique mix of music and humor; then he delivers an inspirational speech that these young people will probably never forget. He starts this speech by falling down on his chest. While he looks up at the crowd, he asks them a very simple question, "What do you do when you fall down?" For most of us, the answer is obvious. You get back up. But when Nick asks the question, the audience is not so sure. Nervous laughter fills the room as he continues to press the question. At this point, Nick becomes more serious and says, "There are times in life when you fall down and don't have the strength to get back up." He continues. "When I fall down, face down with no arms or legs, it should be impossible for me to get up. But it is not."

He goes on to explain, "I will try 100 times to get up, and if I fail 100 times, it does not matter if I fail and try again, and again and again. It is not the end. It only matters how you are going to finish." He then proceeds to show them how he gets back up, with no arms or legs. Here is a person with every reason in the world to give up and yet he spends his time teaching other people how to get back up again.

I often think of Nick and remind myself that I am very fortunate for the gifts God has given me. If you really think about it, Nick is right. Most of us have no excuse for not succeeding in life. You just have to work hard and be ready to take advantage of the opportunities life brings you.

I also find it interesting when people complain about how lucky other people are. When I hear this, I always think of a TV interview that Danny Manning gave right after he had just led the University of Kansas to an NCAA basketball championship. The reporter asked him if he felt lucky to have beaten a team many considered much better than Kansas. Manning simply replied, "Luck is where preparation meets opportunity." Manning knew what most people never learn — we create most of the "luck" in our lives through hard work and preparation.

[2] For more information about Nick, please go to www.attitudeisaltitude.com or www.lifewithoutlimbs.org

If professional success is your goal, then be the first to work, the last to leave, apply yourself, and always take pride in your work. It is true that hard work cleanses the soul. If you want to set yourself apart from the competition, a solid work ethic is a great differentiator. Doing a good job will also help you gain the personal confidence needed to reach out and strive for greater things.

Most of all, this period of my life taught me that life is a journey that starts with the first step. It is a good idea to have a plan, but more often than not, the plans we make rarely determine where we end up in life. The paths we choose and the decisions we make along the way determine where our lives take us. You must believe in yourself and have the courage to take that first step.

Start with accepting responsibility for your life. Understand that from this point forward, you are who you want to be. Do not let anyone make that decision for you, either by how they have treated you or their opinion of what you should be. Too often their judgment will be skewed by the only thing they have for comparison — themselves. It is your life and you have to live it.

The next step is to make sure you truly understand what is important in your life. Success is a recipe made from numerous ingredients. You should sit down and make a list of all the ingredients that are important to you. Faith, family, financial wealth, and educational pursuits are all but a few of the great many things you need to consider. Just remember that with each of these ingredients, there will be trade-offs and sacrifices that need to be made. It does not mean you can't have it all; you just may not be able to have all of everything you want. Prioritize your list of ingredients and make sure you keep it handy. There will be times in your life when you may have to sacrifice one ingredient for another; but never forget what is really important. For me, there is nothing more important than faith, family, and friends.

Finally, you have to be realistic about your talents and abilities. We are all born with certain physical, intellectual, and sensory talents. One of our greatest challenges in life is to understand the breadth of our talents without compromising our potential. On the one hand, you must be realistic about your abilities, but you will never achieve your true potential without high expectations. It is a very difficult distinction to make. But consider this: It is much better to reach for the stars and fall short than to never reach at all.

I have learned that people rise or fall to whatever expectation is set for them. Therefore, set your expectations high and have faith in yourself to achieve them, but temper your life with the understanding that some of our greatest successes come from what we have learned from the losses that came before them. Once you understand this, you will discover there are not many real failures in your life.

Some of the best dishes I have made have come from recipes that have evolved over time. Each time I make a dish, I will add, subtract, or increase the various ingredients until I get it just the way I want it. That is probably the main reason why I enjoy cooking so much — the challenge of making something better than it was before. Life really is a lot like cooking; with a good recipe and the right ingredients, you can make almost anything you want. The ingredients that helped me through this period of life were part of the "roux" that brought me to where I am today. So take that first step, have faith in yourself, and be prepared to work hard to achieve what you really want in life.

Crawfish & Andouille Sausage Gumbo

There are no hard and fast rules for making gumbo beyond the basic roux, okra, and your imagination. The most important part of the gumbo is to form a really dark, rich roux that you will use as a base. Without the right foundation, your Gumbo will be nothing more than a pot of boiled seafood and vegetables. I highly recommend you use a black iron skillet to make your roux. The weight and density of the iron allows the skillet to retain and evenly distribute the heat. I prefer crawfish gumbo, but you can substitute just about any seafood, such as shrimp, crabs, or scallops. I also like to spice my Gumbo up a bit using hot cherry peppers, but this is one of those dishes that you can add or subtract almost anything and it will still taste great (even squirrels!).

Ingredients:

2 lb crawfish with heads attached (can substitute prawns)
½ lb andouille smoked sausage cut in ¾" lengths
1 lb lump crabmeat
1 large yellow onion, quartered
1 large yellow onion, chopped
3 cloves garlic, quartered
4 cloves of garlic, minced
2 stalks of celery, chopped
2 stalks of celery split
1 green bell pepper, chopped
4 medium sized tomatoes, chopped
1 lb okra, sliced in ½" lengths
8 hot cherry peppers, chopped
1 teaspoon fresh thyme
3 bay leaves
1 cup chicken broth
½ cup red wine
2 teaspoons Tabasco sauce
3 tablespoons tomato paste
½ cup canola oil
½ cup all-purpose flour
2 tablespoons Creole seasoning mix
Salt & pepper
2 cups of cooked white rice

Directions:

Carefully remove the meat from the tail of the crawfish and store in refrigerator for use later. Place remaining heads and shells in large pot with 8 cups of water. Add quartered onion, quartered garlic, and split celery stalks.

Place on high heat and bring to boil, and then reduce to simmer uncovered for at least 2 hours.

Using a colander, separate solids from the stock and discard solids. Return stock to the pot. Add chicken broth as necessary to make at least 6 cups of liquid.

Pre-heat a large heavy pan (preferably a cast iron skillet) on high heat. Add sausage and brown on all sides. Remove sausage and set aside, leaving grease from the sausage in the pan.

Add oil. When oil starts to smoke, carefully add the flour while whisking it into the oil. Continue whisking until the roux turns dark brown (about 6-8 minutes).

Add the chopped onion, chopped celery, bell pepper, minced garlic, and hot cherry peppers. Stir constantly until vegetables are softened and lightly browned (about 3-5 minutes). Add Creole mix, then deglaze with red wine, and reduce heat to simmer.

Bring stock in pot to a boil, and then slowly add in the roux mix with vegetables. Stir thoroughly until all of the roux mix is absorbed by the stock, add the sausage, tomatoes, tomato paste, okra, thyme, bay leaves, tobasco sauce, and salt & pepper to taste.

When Gumbo begins to boil, reduce heat to low and cook for at least one hour.

Add the crawfish tails and lump crabmeat and let simmer for 15 minutes. Season to taste with salt, black pepper, and cayenne pepper. Remove bay leaves.

Serve in a bowl over white rice.

RECIPE #3:

EATING PIE WITH A FORK

The Essential Ingredient:
Respect the differences of others

My mother taught me from an early age to be receptive and understanding of other people and their cultures. She called it "eating pie with a fork." Whenever we would visit someone's home, she would always remind us to remember our manners and respect our hosts. If they serve fried chicken, wait and see how they eat it. If they pick it up and eat with their fingers, then you should do the same. If they use a fork and knife, then so should you. She went on to say that if they serve pie, wait and see if they pick up their spoon or fork. If they eat pie with a fork, then you should eat your pie with a fork. As we headed out the door on the way to someone's home, mother would always say, "Don't forget to eat your pie with a fork." That was her way of saying — respect other people for their differences.

There is so much we can learn from other people, and the benefits are enormous. I have always believed that true personal growth is a direct result of what we aspire to learn from the world around us. All it takes is an open mind and an open heart.

But how do you do that? It starts with changing the paradigms that define your perspective about others. You have to eliminate preconceived notions, keeping an open mind to the possibility that you can learn something of value from every person that you meet. You must simply respect their differences and be willing to understand their perspective.

While I was in high school I was asked by my church youth group leader to help organize a basketball game for a relatively new organization that helped the mentally challenged called Special Olympics. She knew I loved basketball, so she asked me to coach one of the men's teams. She also knew I was very competitive; so she reminded me to be patient and let them have fun. That is what I attempted to do, but with a minute left in the game, both teams were tied and we had the ball. My players must have shot the ball at least six times in the final minute and missed every basket. I really wanted my team to win and I was disappointed when the buzzer went off and the game ended in a tie.

But then something amazing happened. The players from both teams started jumping up and down, cheering for each other. I asked one of my players what was going on and he said, "Isn't this great coach, everybody won!" I still get choked up when I think about that moment. Here I was, thinking we had lost, when in reality, I simply had the wrong perspective. It took a Special Olympics athlete to teach me a very valuable lesson. I have been an active supporter of this program ever since.

I learned something very important that day from a very special athlete - winning does not always mean finishing first. Sometimes it just means accomplishing something in spite of all the odds against you. It means getting up every day and doing the very best you can. This is one of the many reasons I believe that success is a very personal thing that must be defined on very personal terms, based on your abilities and talents. If you ever want a testimony from someone on what success looks and feels like, just ask anybody who has witnessed a Special Olympian cross the finish line.

Over the course of my life, I have traveled around the world and had the privilege of experiencing many different cultures. I always make a point of getting away from the crowds and seeking out the experiences of the local community. While I believe there is a basic goodness in all people, our cultural, social, and religious norms vary widely. The greatest mistake most people make is not respecting local cultures when they travel abroad. We falsely assume the rest of the world is just like us and that they only speak a different language. This could not be further from the truth.

Many years ago, I met a retired executive named Frank McGuire, who traveled the country coaching and mentoring CEO's. In his past life, Frank was a senior marketing executive with Federal Express in the company's early days. His job was to sell the new concept of "absolutely, positively overnight" delivery to international markets. Frank would recount countless, sometimes funny, stories about trying to sell this concept to different cultures. Once they went to Sweden and briefed a local business leader about their new overnight delivery service. After they finished the presentation, the Swedish gentlemen leaned back, smiled, and said to them, "That is what's wrong with you Americans. You put everything off until the last minute. If I wanted something to be somewhere tomorrow, I would have sent it two days ago."

Frank's experiences show that my mother's lesson goes well beyond table manners. It speaks to how you should strive to successfully interact in a diverse and constantly changing world.

My mother's lesson on "how to eat pie with a fork" was forged from an era when families actually used to dine together. Dinner was a time when families gathered and shared the stories of the day. Today, most families rarely dine together, and when they do it's too often in front of a TV. There are still places in this world where dining is more than just filling your appetite. It is a time to reflect, entertain and enjoy the company of others. I believe the Italian families know this best of all.

Before we ever visited Italy, we were taught the proper way to dine by an Italian chef from Little Italy in New York City. Fortunately, my mother's words were ringing in my ears as we set off on this particular journey.

Many years ago, on our first trip to New York City, we met John "Cha Cha" Ciarcia who owns a small Italian restaurant on Mulberry Street in the Little Italy section of Manhattan called "Cha Cha's in Bocca Al Lupo Outdoor Cafe." Karen's Uncle knew Cha Cha and suggested we try his restaurant. He said it was located on Mulberry Street just north of Canal Street, and to make sure that we ask for Cha Cha when we get there.

Quite frankly, when we arrived in New York City, we completely forgot about Cha Cha's restaurant, but we had set aside an afternoon to visit China Town. Having never been to New York before, and not knowing where to go, we asked our taxi driver to drop us off on Canal Street "near the shopping area." As fate would have it, he dropped us off on the corner of Canal Street and Mulberry. It was getting close to lunch, and I remembered the restaurant that Karen's Uncle recommended. So we turned up Mulberry Street and went to look for it.

We found the restaurant about 100 yards up on the left, and I have to admit it was not what we expected. It was a real hole-in-the-wall with a narrow entrance and rough exterior that was lined with cheap plastic tables and chairs. I could instantly tell that Karen was not comfortable staying, but we ventured in just the same. One of the servers greeted us and I told him we were here to see Cha Cha. When I told him our name, he lit up and exclaimed, "Cha Cha is expecting you. He is not here yet, but he wants us to make you anything you want."

I looked at Karen and could see in her eyes she did not want to stay; yet, it would not have been polite to leave. We followed our waiter to the back of the restaurant where we were seated.

The back of the restaurant was not much better than the front. It would be generous to call it "rustic." Every inch of the walls were covered with pictures of celebrities, accompanied by a short, dark-haired and very heavy-set man who resembled an extra in an Italian mob movie. We had to assume this was Cha Cha.

The waiter came back and asked me what my favorite dish was and I replied "Veal Parmigiana." He said, "Fine. I will bring you the best Veal Parmigiana you have ever had."

When the food finally came out, we were pleasantly surprised. It was one of the best Veal Parmigiana I had ever eaten. The veal was crisp on the outside and perfectly tender on the inside, and the red sauce was simply fantastic. It was clearly not what we expected.

We had just finished lunch when Cha Cha arrived with his wife, who coincidentally is also named Karen. Cha Cha was wearing an old chef's jacket with baggy "bakers" pants. He pulled up a chair and began to speak.

Cha Cha was pretty much everything you would have expected from his pictures. He was a rough and gruff guy who seemed to have little use for small talk and normal pleasantries, but he also had a certain charm about him I liked. He told it like it was, or at least how he thought it should be.

We talked for about an hour, mostly about his passion for food, and he was passionate about food! He was on a quest that day to create the perfect pistachio gelato, which is an Italian version of ice cream. It was getting late and I had made a reservation that night at one of the best restaurants in town, so we had to excuse ourselves. As we were getting ready to leave, I thanked him for the meal, which he refused to let us pay for.

Before we made it to the curb, Cha Cha's wife, Karen, came running out and stopped us. She said, "Cha Cha really liked meeting you."

I said, "Thank you. I enjoyed meeting him as well."

She replied, "You don't understand. Cha Cha really liked you, and he does not normally like people until he gets to know them. He wants to take you out to dinner tonight."

I looked at my wife and there was that look again. I had already pressed my luck by dragging her into this restaurant and then actually eating there, not to mention the fact that I was supposed to take her shopping; but we spent most of the afternoon talking food with Cha Cha instead. Then she did something that completely surprised me. She turned to Karen and said, "Sure, we'd love to." I was flabbergasted.

I asked Cha Cha's wife where they wanted to go, and she said, "Don't worry about it. Cha Cha will take you to the best restaurant in Little Italy. We will see you at 8."

I have to admit I was not real happy that Karen agreed to this. It was Saturday night on our first trip to New York City. I had made reservations at a famous restaurant. I had even arranged for a private driver for the evening, and Karen had picked out a spectacular outfit to wear that night. I had to keep reminding myself we were going to visit "the best restaurant in Little Italy."

We arrived in front of Cha Cha's restaurant at 8 p.m. sharp. There was Cha Cha waiting for us, still wearing the same old chef's jacket and baggy pants from earlier that day. The only difference was that he was now covered with flour from cooking all afternoon in his kitchen. This was not starting out like we had hoped. We were all dressed up, and there was obviously no place to go, but we were in for a big surprise.

Cha Cha walked toward the street and said, "Follow me."

We made it about the length of one storefront when a shopkeeper came running out and grabbed Cha Cha's hand, greeting him with the respect one would usually afford a dignitary. The shopkeeper reached out with both hands, with a slightly bowed head, and shook Cha Cha's hand while saying, "It's good to see you Mr. Cha Cha."

Mr. Cha Cha? What is this about? No sooner did we get a little further down the street than someone else came up and greeted him in a similar fashion. As it turned out, just about everyone on the street that evening seemed to know who he was, and one by one they came over to greet him. Then it dawned on me. We may be walking down the street with a real life Tony Soprano! He certainly looked and talked like one, but little did we know we were walking down the middle of Mulberry Street with the "unofficial" Mayor of Little Italy.

We stopped in front of a restaurant named Il Cortile and there was a crowd waiting out front to be seated. The owner had spotted Cha Cha as we were walking down the street and ran out to meet us. He said, "Cha Cha, I have your table waiting for you."

He took us through the restaurant to the very back where the room opened up to a high ceiling. There in the middle was a table already set up with wine and a large tray of antipasto. Cha Cha was clearly the center of attention as every waiter, and almost every patron of the restaurant came over to greet him.

After we were seated, a waiter came out to fill our glasses with wine. I asked him if he was going to bring us some menus. The waiter looked up at Cha Cha, turned to me with a smile, and then walked away. I was not sure what had just happened. Cha Cha said,

"Tonight you will learn to eat like a true Italian. There will be no menus. Just lots of food and lots of fun."

That was the night we first learned what it meant to dine Italian style. Italians take their food very seriously, but eating is a leisurely experience that requires a mixture of patience and restraint. Quite simply, there is no rush, there will be a lot of food, and sharing is an important part of the experience.

They started with a series of appetizers, which Italian's refer to as antipasti. They brought us several trays of sliced meats, cheeses, and vegetables that had been roasted, then chilled and marinated in olive oil. As soon as one tray was emptied, another would quickly appear with some new delicacy. I was like a kid in a candy shop.

After about an hour or so, the waiter appeared and asked us what kind of pasta we liked. Everyone told him his or her favorite pasta dish, and off he went to the kitchen. Karen and I thought we were ordering our dinner, but little did we know we were about to be introduced to the first course of a traditional Italian dinner – primo di pasta.

About 30 minutes later, the waiter arrived with stacks of large bowls filled with the different pastas we ordered. The dishes included massive servings of penne Arrabbiata, spaghetti Bolognese, and fettuccini with a white wine and clam sauce. For the next several hours, we dined like the ancient Romans; the wine kept flowing, and we were having the time of our lives.

When the waiter finally returned, it was well past 10 p.m. and we were stuffed to the gills. He looked at Cha Cha and said, "How about I bring you a nice Three Musketeer?" I assumed he was talking about dessert, but again I was wrong.

Another 30 minutes went by when the waiter brought out a large tray filled with Veal Chops, Chicken Scaloppini and Veal Saltimbocca. It was then we learned what a "Three Musketeer" really meant — three courses of meat. We also learned that the main course in a traditional Italian meal is the second course, which is referred to as secondo. The secondo usually consists of meat and poultry (secondi di carni e volatili) or seafood (pescato di mare). He also brought out a series of side dishes, which are called contorni. Contorni's also include salad, which unlike American-style dining, is served at the very end of the meal.

We had never eaten so much in one seating, but the food was fantastic and Cha Cha was entertaining us with the stories of his life. Remember all of those pictures on the walls of his restaurant? Those were friends and associates of Cha Cha from his many years as a boxing promoter, consultant, and extra in mob movies. Cha Cha told us the story of how, many years before, he discovered and promoted a young boxer named Tony Danza who went on to star in the TV sitcom, "Taxi." In the famous mob movie, "Goodfellas," Cha Cha was part of the movie's most memorable scene; he played a member of Billy Batts' crew. Cha Cha was sitting next to Billy Batts when the memorable line, "Go get your shinebox," was uttered. He has since been involved in dozens of movies and television shows such as "The Sopranos." Cha Cha was also the producer of the film "Mamamia" which won "Best Short Film Award" at the New York International Independent Film & Video Festival in which Tony Danza directed and starred.

This was a night of lessons and memories — a lesson to never judge a book by its cover, let alone a person or a restaurant. We also learned how to dine like a true Italian, as they have done for centuries since the times of the Romans, and we created memories of the greatest meal I have ever enjoyed before or since.

Now it was really getting late. The waiter came out with a small tray of fruits and cheeses that are known as *dolce*. Interestingly enough, dessert is not often eaten in Italy, as Romans by and large did not have a big sweet tooth. I have to agree with the Romans, since I have never been a big fan of dessert.

The waiter also offered us a selection of *caffe* or a "digestive" (after dinner drink). Traditionally, coffee is not served until after the meal, and it is always a *caffe*, never a sugar and cream-laced cappuccino. *Caffe* is believed to have the effect of capping the flavors of the feast and suppressing the appetite until the next meal.

No true Italian dining experience is complete, however, without a good digestive, and the most traditional of all is *grappa*. *Grappa* is a uniquely Italian drink made from the discarded grape seeds, stalks, and stems that are the by-product of the winemaking process.

This night would be our first experience with *grappa*, and I have to warn you that *grappa* is an acquired taste. That first sip almost tasted like turpentine, but once I got the hang of it, I was hooked. The key is to serve it chilled in a small glass and sip it slowly. Years later, as we traveled around Italy, we discovered that some Italians like to mix a little *grappa* in their *espresso* at the end of the meal. It really takes the bite out of the *grappa*.

That one evening completely changed our perspective on dining. Later that year, we visited Italy for the first time and have been back several times since. There could have been no better training for dining in Italy than a night with Cha Cha. Now when we visit any Italian restaurant here or abroad, we tell our server that we plan to eat "Italian style"— one course at a time, sharing each dish, and taking our time to do so. You have to make this clear as soon as you sit down. Too many American restaurants try to get you to place your entire order up front, pushing the food through too quickly so they can turn the table over. Many Americans are accustomed to this form of dining. The "Italian style" of dining is so much more relaxed and, besides, you get to try more things on the menu.

As a tribute to Cha Cha, and all of the other great Italian restaurants that we have found over the years, I have organized my recipes in the order they should be served. While many of my recipes are not Italian dishes, they are all prepared with the same method and, most of all, love. If there is one thing I have learned from Italian chefs it's that cooking is an expression of love that is best served "Italian style" — one course at a time, sharing each dish, and enjoying the moment with the people you truly care about.

The essence of "eating pie with a fork" is to learn to respect and understand the differences in others. Even across our great nation, there are countless local and regional influences that shape the way people think and how they interact with each other. You will find the world we live in will be much easier to navigate if you have a healthy respect for the differences in others. In fact, our world would be a much better place if we could all learn to eat pie with a fork.

Veal Parmigiana

Veal Parmigiana is one of my favorite dishes. This Southern Italian dish is traditionally made with fried thin sliced veal, layered with cheese and tomato sauce, then baked. I prefer to prepare meat with the bone in for the added flavor. I also prefer to directly hand-rub the veal with the seasoning rather than mixing them with the breadcrumbs. In this particular version, I butterfly veal rib chops, pound them out real thin, and hand rub them with a light dusting of paprika, garlic powder, salt and pepper. Finally, I prepare my Veal Milanese style, with the cheese mixed into the breadcrumbs as opposed to melting the cheese on top. The result is a very flavorful and crispy Veal Parmigiana, and I recommend you serve this directly over a bed of my marinara sauce with pasta on the side. This dish is a tribute to my friend Cha Cha for teaching me the joy of dining Italian Style!

Ingredients:
4 veal rib chops
1 cup Italian bread crumbs
¼ cup reggiano parmesan
¼ chopped Italian parsley
2 eggs beaten with 1 teaspoon water
¼ cup olive oil
Paprika, garlic powder, salt and pepper
4 cups of marinara sauce (see recipe)

Directions:
Starting at the end of the bone, butterfly the veal rib chops evenly down the middle. Then cover the veal with plastic wrap and pound

out meat using a meat hammer.

Hand rub the veal with paprika, garlic powder, salt & pepper. Let stand for at least 30 minutes at room temperature.

Combine bread crumbs, cheese, and parsley in a large bowl. Crack eggs into another large bowl. Mix in water and whip until thoroughly mixed.

Pre-heat oven to 450 degrees.

In a pre-heated pan on high heat, add 2 tablespoons of oil. Note: as you brown the veal, make sure you add just enough oil to coat the bottom of the pan.

Dip veal in egg and cover with bread and cheese mix.

Brown veal on each side for no more that 2 minutes; then place on baking sheet.

Finish in oven for 5-10 minutes.

Serve over bed of marinara sauce.

RECIPE #4:
"THE MOST IMPORTANT INGREDIENT"

The Essential Ingredient:
Stand up for what is right

As I said at the very beginning, living a great life requires a great recipe, and a great recipe is more than just selecting the right ingredients and mixing them together. You have to start with a vision of what you want to create, select the right ingredients, measure carefully, and prepare them in the proper order to create something truly special. As simple as this may sound, it is actually quite difficult. It takes many attempts of trial and error to figure out your recipe, and with each attempt there will be difficult choices that need to be made.

The hardest decisions that you will make are the ones that test your character and challenge you to choose between doing what is right versus what is convenient. Unfortunately, the path of convenience is almost always the easier path to take. Just remember that if you use convenience as one of your ingredients, you probably will not like the way your dish turns out. A great life requires a great recipe and a great recipe requires the right ingredients; the most important ingredient of all is learning how to do the right things for the right reasons.

That is why it is so important to have a "moral compass" in your life. A moral compass is the one thing you rely on to measure whether or not you are headed in the right direction. Your values will guide you through the many challenges you encounter throughout your life. Without these guiding values, it becomes too easy to do what feels good, rather than what is actually good for you.

God is my moral compass. While I admit to not being an

overtly religious person, I do have a very deep and personal spiritual relationship with God. Whether or not you believe in God, the lessons the Bible teaches will help you figure out how to do the right things and, in doing so, you will find life much more rewarding.

This is why our founding fathers used Judeo-Christian principles as the foundation of our system of government. They clearly understood how important it was for a society to be based on a system of laws that represent morality and justice. If you ask most Americans what type of government we have, they will likely tell you that we live in a democracy. A democracy by definition is a system of government that relies on the rule of the majority. Our forefathers, however, had something much better in mind when they created our system of government. They wanted to create a republic — a government based on a system of laws that ensures the rights of all its citizens regardless of their race, religion, sex, or national creed. They based these laws on the Judeo-Christian principles of the Old and New Testaments of the Bible.

I find it interesting that so many people spend so much emotional energy arguing the constitutionality of the separation of church and state, yet they overlook our founding fathers' true and most precious intentions - they wanted to create a society with specific freedoms, such as the freedom of religion, but they never intended to create a system of laws that was free from the morality of a universal God. They created a recipe for our country that included the most important of all ingredients: doing the right things for the right reasons; they called it our Constitution.

Doing the right things for the right reasons can be very difficult. There will be sacrifices along the way, both personal and professional. But rest assured, these sacrifices are well worth knowing that you did your best while subscribing to a greater good. More importantly, as I look back on my life, it was these sacrifices that ultimately turned out to be opportunities that became the essential ingredients in my recipe for success.

I was introduced to one of these "opportunities" soon after I left the oil fields of Louisiana. At the time, I realized that unless I wanted to spend the rest of my life doing manual labor, I needed a good education. So I moved back to Cleveland and took a night job selling clothes at a local mall. I planned to enroll in the fall semester at a local community college.

It was here that I met another person who changed my life. Bob Szalay and I met while we were both managers for a hip new chain of clothing stores. We were having the time of our lives running these stores and traveling around the country, hiring and training employees for new stores. We were having so much fun that I did not enroll in school like I had planned.

Bob had bigger ideas for me. He wanted me to join the Air Force with him under the "buddy program," during which we would go to basic training together and have the same assignment. He knew I wanted to go to college and he was convinced that the Air Force was the way to get me there. At that time, I had no desire to join the military, but I let Bob talk me into taking the entrance exam and meeting his recruiter. I scored very well on the exams, but that only made Bob and his recruiter more determined to get me to join. I knew in my heart Bob was right. The longer I stayed in my current situation, the less likely I would ever go to school. A week later, Bob and I joined the Air Force.

The recruiter promised us we would go to basic training together, attend the same technical school, and be assigned to the same base. More importantly, the military would help me get my college education. Bob and I went down to the Armed Forces Enlistment Station, took our oaths, and we never saw each other again. They literally sent us to opposite ends of the world.

I am certainly not the first person who was ever lied to by a military recruiter, but it turned out to be one of the best things that could ever have happened to me. Although I never saw Bob again, he put me on a path that changed my life. Bob, like many others in my life who came both before and after him, saw something in me much bigger than working in a clothing store. I just needed to be properly motivated to listen and act on their advice.

So off to basic training I went.

The fundamental goal of military basic training is to strip down enlistees, remove their individuality, and rebuild them as a team. On the first day of basic training, they shaved our heads, stripped us of all our possessions, and put us into groups of eight people called "patrols." Among other things, they taught us how to march, stand in formation, salute, and make our beds. As menial as these tasks appeared, everything we did was in unison and was all about working together as a team.

From each patrol group, they randomly assigned one of us to be the "patrol leader." The patrol leader was responsible for leading his group through daily training exercises. If the team failed to achieve their objectives, the Drill Sergeants would remove the patrol leader and assign the job to someone else in the group. About once a week the entire patrol leader staff in a squadron would typically be removed and reassigned.

I was assigned the patrol leader position on the very first day of basic training. One of my first tasks was to take my patrol to the personnel office to "select" our career field. When our group arrived at the personnel office, we were ushered into a large theater with about 100 other young men. Shortly thereafter, a young sergeant walked in and asked everyone who joined the military without a specific job assignment to raise our hands. About 80 of us raised our hands, including everyone in my patrol. Most of us believed our recruiters when they encouraged us to not ask for a specific job assignment before we left for basic training. They told us we would be able to make a better decision once we had a taste of military life. But the sergeant explained it a little differently to us. He said our recruiters had lied to us and the Air Force would decide what job we would get. When one of our guys remarked that he had been promised a job in "electronics," the sergeant told him that means he might get a job "screwing light bulbs in igloos." We were simply devastated. I don't think any of us slept much that night.

The next morning, I made the decision to go back to the personnel office to get this straightened out. When I told my patrol what I was going to do, they told me I was crazy. As a basic trainee, you learn very quickly to never question any authority. It was pretty likely I would be demoted, spending the rest of my miserable basic training experience peeling potatoes; but there was simply too much at stake.

When I arrived at the personnel center, I asked for the person in charge and was directed to the Senior Master Sergeant for the entire facility. Now keep in mind that I was a nothing in this military world and here I was standing in front of the second-highest ranking enlisted person on the entire base. But, at that point, I had nothing to lose.

I explained to him what the sergeant told us the day before and then I asked him a question. "How can I expect my guys to do anything I tell them if the first lesson they learn is to never believe anyone with authority?" Fortunately, I was standing in front of someone who stood for something more than just procedures. Within two days, everyone in our patrol got a personal appointment with a career counselor, and they were able to pick their own career field. The Senior Master Sergeant also recommended me for an elite technical training program that I later learned would change my life.

Over the next 12 weeks of basic training, I was the only patrol leader in our squadron who kept his job the entire time we were there. The only reason I kept my job is because my team never let me down. They taught me a very important lesson – if you take care of your team, they will take care of you.

Throughout my life, I have recalled that pivotal moment and asked myself where I would be today if I had not stood up for my team. I cannot imagine an outcome better than the path my decisions have led me.

There will be many opportunities in your life to stand up and do the right thing. Some of these will come at great personal risk and sacrifice, but I can guarantee you that life is so much more fulfilling when you can look at yourself in the mirror and know you did your best to do the right thing.

There will be just as many times in your life when you will witness an injustice that may not directly affect you. Do not allow yourself to believe you have no responsibility to others. Some of the world's greatest tragedies occurred under the tacit acceptance of masses of people who were either too scared to stand up or allowed themselves to believe it was not their problem. To paraphrase Sir Edmund Burke, an 18th-century British statesman, all that is necessary for the forces of evil to triumph is for enough good men to do nothing. When faced with injustice, you only have the choice to approve or disapprove, and sometimes the greatest form of approval is silence. So speak out on what you believe.

It may come as a surprise to most people who have not served in the military that our soldiers, sailors, airmen and marines are not just trained to follow orders. From the very beginning we are taught the traditions of duty, honor, and courage. Just as important, we are taught the difference between lawful and unlawful orders. I believe one of the many things that set the American military apart from many others around the world is our belief that there is a right way and a wrong way to do things, even in times of war. We are taught to choose the right way, even if it comes at great personal sacrifice.

My military experience taught me a great appreciation for those who serve. I admit I did not join the military out of a sense of duty to my country. I did it because I wanted to get an education. But along the way, I developed a strong sense of patriotism that only service can teach. Without a doubt, the best part of being in the military was having the privilege to serve with some of the finest people I have ever met in my life. These individuals put their lives on the line for things that most of us take for granted, such as freedom and opportunity. I had the privilege of meeting one of my personal heroes, Medal of Honor recipient Col. Bud Day, who was shot down over Vietnam, escaped twice, and was severely beaten and tortured. I also met many others like him who have given a significant part of their lives, working long hours for low pay, to protect our country.

Some of our real and too often unsung heroes are the families they leave behind. There are countless fathers, mothers, husbands, wives, sons, and daughters who sacrifice so much on a daily basis so that their loved ones could properly execute their duties.

I believe serving others is the greatest form of love. People who excel in these fields have a passion for people. This is true not just in the military, but in our hospitals, fire departments, police agencies, social services, community charities, and even the restaurants and hotels we visit.

Years later, I was asked to speak at a leadership conference; I wanted to share my leadership experiences with the group on a very personal level. I thought back to the leadership lessons I learned during my military service. I thought about the people who helped me get through basic training, obtain my education, and improve my career. I realized the best leaders I ever had were the ones who took the time to teach me and supported me when I needed them the most. I wanted to illustrate the point of "standing up for what is right and taking care of your team," so I took one slide with me — an organizational chart for the group I was getting ready to address. It was your typical organizational chart with the boss' name and title in a box on the top and a series of boxes below, showing all of the people who worked for that person. I put it on the slide projector and said, "If you want to know everything about being a good leader, just remember this." I then turned the slide upside down with the boss on the bottom and everyone else above. I said, "Great leaders take care of their people and, as a result, their people take care of them."

Smoked Baby Back Ribs with Marks Cajun BBQ Sauce

This is the very first recipe I wrote. I have been fascinated with making ribs as far back as I can remember. Maybe it was because some of my favorite childhood memories were family gatherings in the backyard around a rusty old charcoal grill. Years later I developed a BBQ restaurant concept that won quite a few awards and BBQ contests.

Most people don't realize that BBQ has a unique relationship to Cajun culture. In the early 19th century, food was scarce and wild hogs were abundant in the backwoods and swamps of southern Louisiana. It took a lot of work to capture and cook these wild hogs, so pig hunting was a team-effort, and the neighborhood would be invited to share in the feast. In Cajun culture, these are called "boucheries", which are sometimes also called 'pig-pickin's.' The traditional Southern barbecue grew out of these gatherings. Hence why I chose this recipe for this chapter – BBQ comes from tradition of doing the right things and taking care of your neighbors.

As BBQ spread across the south, each region laid claim to its own particular variety of barbecue, particularly as it relates to their sauce. There are four basic barbecue sauces that represent each region, including mustard-based, vinegar-based, ketchup-based, and tomato-based sauces. There are also endless varieties of sauces created by combining two or more of these basic ingredients.

*There are three requirements for a great BBQ rib: 1) a good rub that is applied at least one day before you cook; 2) slow cooking the ribs (preferably with a smoker); and, 3) the sauce. The ribs should never "fall off the bone" when you eat them. Properly smoked and grilled, they will develop an almost pink color and will stay firmly attached to the bone. As noted below, I make my own sauce and rub from scratch. My sauce actually blends the basic ingredients of all four types of sauces, and the unique flavor of my sauce comes from using **the most important ingredient** – burnt onions!*

The secret to this sauce is burning a portion of the onions and adding them to create a smoky flavor and an interesting crunchy texture to the sauce. Burning something is counterintuitive to most chefs' instincts, so you really have to understand what I mean by burning the onions - burn them to a crisp until the onions turn into charcoal. I recommend you use a black iron skillet, and you may want to do this outside because it will throw off a lot of smoke. I usually make a very large batch that will last several months and refrigerate it in a sealed container. This sauce also makes a great gift for your family and friends.

Ingredients for the sauce:

1 white onion, diced and separated into two even piles
3 cloves garlic, sliced
32 oz of tomato ketchup (see recipe)
½ cup brown molasses
½ cup red wine
3 tablespoons olive oil
¼ cup yellow mustard
3 teaspoons Tabasco sauce
3 tablespoons lemon juice
2 tablespoons Worchester sauce
1 teaspoon crushed red pepper
Cayenne pepper
Salt & pepper

Directions for the sauce:

In a large saucepan, heat tomato ketchup with molasses, Tabasco, cayenne pepper, mustard, salt, pepper, and lemon juice.

Pre-heat pan on medium to high heat and add 2 tablespoons olive oil. Brown ½ of the onions (about 3-5 minutes), then add garlic and crushed red pepper. Then deglaze with wine and cook until reduced (about 3 minutes). Add to sauce.

In the same pan, turn heat to high and add remaining olive oil. Add remaining onion and cook until blackened (it must be as black and hard as charcoal). Add to the sauce.

Cook until thickened and let simmer for at least 1 hour.

Ingredients for the ribs:

2 racks baby back ribs, 1-½ to 2 pounds each

4-5 tablespoons BBQ rub (see recipe)

2 cups BBQ sauce (see recipe)

2 cups wood chips, soaked in water for at least 1 hour

Directions for the ribs:

One day prior to cooking ribs, generously rub each rack with BBQ rub, pressing the spices into the meat. Tightly wrap racks with plastic wrap and refrigerate. Allow the ribs to stand at room temperature for 20 to 30 minutes before grilling.

Drain the wood chips and toss them directly onto the burning coals or into the smoker box of a gas grill, following manufacturer's instructions. Grill the ribs over indirect low heat (grill temperature should be about 300°F), until the meat is very tender and has shrunk back from the ends of the bones, approximately 1 hour.

After the ribs are done, start brushing occasionally with the sauce on both sides and grill until crispy.

Transfer the ribs to a sheet pan and tightly cover with aluminum foil. Let rest for 30 minutes. Serve warm.

RECIPE #5:

FINDING FRESH INGREDIENTS

The Essential Ingredient:
Recognize the "angels" in your life

Everything we do, everyone we meet, and everything we experience becomes the ingredients that create our recipe for life. If you want to improve your recipe, fresh ingredients are key. Some of the best ingredients I have found are the "angels" that came into my life and helped me along the way. I believe the world is full of angels, particularly those angels without wings we call "friends." In fact, my entire life has been guided by various "angels" that stepped in and intervened when I needed it the most. Unfortunately, I rarely, if ever, recognize these "angels" when they are actually affecting my life. It usually happens much later in life when I can reflect and appreciate the positive impact they had.

I wish I could remember the name of that Senior Master Sergeant from basic training, because he turned out to be one of many people who had a tremendous influence on my life. That morning in his office activated a chain of events that led me to where I am today. This is one reason why I have chosen to identify so many of the "angels" I have met over the years, like Gerald and Bob, and thank them for what they have done for me.

One of the keys to success in life is finding and recognizing the "angels" in your life. If you are going to find these "angels," then you need to have an open mind and be receptive to the ideas of others.

As it turned out, the "elite technical training program" this Senior Master Sergeant introduced me to turned out to be a top-secret surveillance program under the Nuclear Detection Agency. It required attending the longest and most academically rigid technical training program in the Air Force. In order to minimize attrition, the

Air Force sent us to a one-month school just to learn how to study and retain information. I was always the child who scored high on aptitude tests but performed poorly in class. However, this one short course changed my learning habits and allowed me to excel at every school I attended from that point forward. I went on to earn four college degrees and graduate at the top of my class. I would never have been able to achieve any of this without the intervention of one person who decided to make a difference in my life.

Another influential "angel" was the head of my youth group at church. Her name was Franny Milward. Franny had an incredible passion for young people and could always see the good in someone, no matter what they did or pretended to be. She scoured the inner city, looking for young people who needed a place to go; I was one of those young people she rescued from the streets and instilled with her faith and trust. From the age of 15 to when I left home, Franny is probably the main reason I did not end up on drugs or in jail. I know I let her down more times than I can count, but she always took me back in and gave me another chance. Eventually, her love and patience took hold, and I graduated high school and moved on to a much better life.

Without a doubt, the most important "angel" in my life is my wife and best friend, Karen. Karen and I met right after I completed my training in the Air Force and was transferred to Cocoa Beach, Fla. Until then, I had been in and out of a lot of relationships, never finding anyone who captured my heart. By the time I met Karen, I was at a point in my life where I had pretty much given up on the idea of having a long-term relationship. We met through a group of friends at a nightclub near the base and spent the entire night sitting together and talking. Before the night was over, I had literally fallen in love with her; however, our relationship almost ended before it ever began. I forgot to ask for her phone number.

During our long conversation that night, Karen said she might stop by the club the following weekend, so I showed up early and sat there all night hoping she would come. It was getting late and I was just about to leave when she walked in. My heart almost jumped through my chest.

Unfortunately, I was also broke. At the time, I was living in the barracks on base and taking home only $80 every two weeks. I couldn't even afford to buy her a drink, but I had a plan that included a cheap bottle of wine and my guitar. We spent that night sitting on the beach and drinking wine; as she listened to me play my guitar. To this day, I have always been surprised that she came with me.

There we were, under the moonlight, with the ocean waves crashing at our feet. It was the most perfect night of my life, but just like the waves, it almost came crashing down. It was getting late, so I offered to take her home. I reached in my pocket to retrieve my car keys, only to find they were missing. We walked back to where we were sitting and searched the area. The moon was full, but the beach was littered with seaweed, which made it nearly impossible to find anything. It was like looking for a needle in a haystack. For the next 30 minutes, I retraced my steps back to the car and I could see that she was starting to get concerned.

Then, halfway between the car and where we were sitting, I dropped to my knees and said, "I will walk on my hands and knees across this entire path until I find them." As soon as my hand hit the sand, it landed on my car keys. I immediately jumped up and announced my discovery, only to see her look at me with profound disappointment spread across her face, clearly suggesting that I did this on purpose. I quietly took her home that night, never expecting to see her again.

This time she gave me her phone number; however, and for the next two days I deliberated whether or not to call her. I finally mustered up the courage to call, and quite surprisingly she agreed to see me again. We had four dates over the next two weeks. A week later, on New Year's Eve, we were engaged. Eight months later, we were married.

Through this experience, I learned another important lesson. You do not always find true love… sometimes it has to find you. Just when I had almost given up on finding the right person, Karen came into my life. From the moment I met her, I knew she was special, but I also knew I had screwed up a lot of previous relationships by trying too hard. That first night we just sat and talked and, as it turned out, this is what attracted Karen to me in the first place. I was not trying to impress her. I was just being myself and having a good time.

If you want true love, you have to make yourself available to be loved. You have to open your soul and trust someone to hold your heart in his or her hands.

Likewise, if you want angels to come into your life, you must make an effort to be someone else's angel.

This requires taking down those barriers that prevent you from connecting with the angels that enter your life. Some of the hardest barriers to overcome are fear, insecurity, and selfishness. You have to feel good about yourself in order to feel good about others. If you can feel good about others, you will attract their good feelings as well. When I met Karen, I was scared to death. I had no money, no formal education, and no position, but she saw something much greater in me and was willing to invest in me with her love.

I knew in my heart the only way I could "repay" her for her investment was to be the person she knew I could be. I made a commitment to myself many years before that I was going to be successful, raise a family, and be a good father. Karen gave me the motivation and purpose to achieve that goal.

There have been plenty of "angels" in my life. Unfortunately, we usually do not recognize them until it is too late. One of the many lessons I have learned from Karen is that we need to treat everyone we meet as a potential "angel." That is certainly her gift in life — to be kind to everyone you meet. And I have to admit - it is hard work. Being kind to others is not always easy, especially in the crazy, high-tech, and ultra high-stress world that we all live in. Without the benefit of true human interaction, it becomes too easy to virtually smack someone with an email. However, kindness has a way of transcending all other forms of communication. Mother Theresa once said, "Kindness is a language we all understand. Even the blind can see it and the deaf can hear it."

All of the "angels" I have met in my life had one thing in common. They all saw something in me that was much greater than even I understood. They believed in me and, through their faith, I gained the personal confidence to achieve so much in my life. One of the greatest recipes for success is to learn to recognize the "angels" who can change your life, and one of the greatest gifts that you can give others is to learn to be an "angel." Use every opportunity to teach, mentor, and coach others to success. The rewards are endless and I believe you will achieve true balance and happiness when you give as much or more than you receive.

If you want to know if you have achieved proper balance in your life, start by making a list of the "angels" in your life and how they helped you along the way. You may even want to thank some of them for their contribution. A simple handwritten note will have a tremendous value to those who have helped you along the way.

Hopefully your list of "angels" is long, but if it is not, it may be a sign that you haven't been paying enough attention to those around you who really want to help you succeed. You should also make a list right next to it of the people you think would consider you as their angel. If that list is short, then you have a lot of work to do. You know you will have achieved balance in your life when both of these lists are long and varied.

It takes both an open heart and an open mind to recognize a potential "angel." Too often we dismiss people without giving them the opportunity to make a difference in our lives. The key is to treat everyone you encounter as a potential "angel" and never assume you know their value without giving them the opportunity to demonstrate it.

More importantly, never underestimate your power to change someone else's life. Kindness and understanding are the most powerful gifts you can bestow on the people you encounter. It takes so little effort to give these gifts to the people in your life. Recently, a friend sent me a very moving story he found on the Internet that really makes this point. The story recounts the experience of a high-school "jock" that befriended a "nerd" and ultimately changed his life without even realizing it. Since I generally distrust anything that is widely circulated on the Internet, I tried to research its origins and verify that it was in fact true. While I could not confirm the facts of this particular story, it was amazing to see how many people read it and recalled similar experiences in their lives. The power of "angels" we call friends is overwhelming, as this story illustrates:

One day, when I was a freshman in high school, I saw a kid from my class walking home from school. His name was Kyle. It looked like he was carrying all of his books. I thought to myself, "Why would anyone bring home all his books on a Friday? He must really be a nerd."

I had quite a weekend planned (parties and a football game with my friends tomorrow afternoon), so I shrugged my shoulders and went on.

As I was walking, I saw a bunch of kids running toward him. They ran at him, knocking all his books out of his arms and tripping him so he landed in the dirt. His glasses went flying and I saw them land in the grass about ten feet from him. He looked up and I saw this terrible sadness in his eyes. My heart went out to him. So, I jogged over to him and as he crawled around looking for his glasses, I saw a tear in his eye. As I handed him his glasses, I said, "Those guys are jerks. They really should get lives."

He looked at me and said, "Hey thanks!" There was a big smile on his face. It was one of those smiles that showed real gratitude.

I helped him pick up his books and asked him where he lived. As it turned out, he lived near me, so I asked him why I had never seen him before. He said he had gone to private school before now. I would have never hung out with a private school kid before. We talked all the way home and I carried some of his books. He turned out to be a pretty cool kid.

I asked him if he wanted to play a little football with my friends. He said yes. We hung out all weekend and the more I got to know Kyle, the more I liked him, and my friends thought the same of him.

Monday morning came and there was Kyle with the huge stack of books again. I stopped him and said, "Boy, you are gonna really build some serious muscles with this pile of books everyday!" He just laughed and handed me half the books.

Over the next four years, Kyle and I became best friends. When we were seniors, we began to think about college. Kyle decided on Georgetown and I was going to Duke. I knew that we would always be friends, that the miles would never be a problem. He was going to be a doctor and I was going for business on a football scholarship. Kyle was valedictorian of our class. I teased him all the time about being a nerd. He had to prepare a speech for graduation. I was so glad it wasn't me having to get up there and speak.

Graduation day, I saw Kyle. He looked great. He was one of those guys that really found himself during high school. He filled out and actually looked good in glasses. He had more dates than I had and all the girls loved him. Boy, sometimes I was jealous.

Today was one of those days. I could see that he was nervous about his speech. So, I smacked him on the back and said, "Hey, big guy, you'll be great!" He looked at me with one of those looks (the really grateful one) and smiled. "Thanks," he said.

As he started his speech, he cleared his throat, and began. "Graduation is a time to thank those who helped you make it through those tough years – your parents, your teachers, your siblings, maybe a coach, but mostly your friends. I am here to tell all of you that being a friend to someone is the best gift you can give them. I am going to tell you a story."

I just looked at my friend with disbelief as he told the story of the first day we met. He had planned to kill himself over the weekend. He talked of how he had cleaned out his locker so his Mom wouldn't have to do it later and was carrying his stuff home. He looked hard at me and gave me a little smile. "Thankfully, I was saved. My friend saved me from doing the unspeakable."

I heard the gasp go through the crowd as this handsome, popular boy told us all about his weakest moment. I saw his Mom and dad looking at me and smiling that same grateful smile. Not until that moment did I realize its depth.

We should never underestimate the power of our actions. With one small gesture, you can change a person's life — for better or for worse. We all have the opportunity to be each other's "angels," impacting one another in some way.

It is a lot easier to recognize the "angels" in your life if you are the kind of person that takes responsibility for your actions, respects the differences in others, and places others before yourself.

You will also be more likely to be given the opportunity to become someone else's "angel." Once that happens, your life will begin to change in ways you could never imagine. People will reach out to you, new opportunities will become available, and your life will become much more satisfying.

Margherita Pizza

*There are not many dishes that are as fun to make with others like creating your own pizza. The secret to making a great pizza is using only **fresh ingredients**, including making your dough from scratch. Believe it or not, the easiest part of making a pizza is making the dough. This is a very basic recipe that produces a good thin-crust pizza when rolled out on a hard surface. It is important to make your dough in advance and allow it to refrigerate for at least 2 hours before setting it out to rise. I find the dough produces a better, crispier crust if I refrigerate it for 24 hours or more (you can even freeze it).*

The best pizzas are made in wood or charcoal-fired ovens. You can replicate this technique with a good pizza stone placed on your outdoor gas or charcoal grill. Most of the popular kitchenware stores sell them for under $50. Place the stone on your already heated grill and allow it to pre-heat for about 20 minutes.

You should also get a "pizza peel" to transfer the pizza to the stone.

Since dough will stick to most surfaces, you should sprinkle corn meal on the pizza peel before applying the dough and pizza ingredients. Also, you can achieve a crispier pizza if you lightly brush the rolled out dough with olive oil before applying any ingredients.

My favorite pizza is a simple Margherita pizza that consists of a thick layer of marinara sauce, followed by a layer of shredded mozzarella with slices of vine-ripe tomatoes and fresh basil on top of the cheese. But the best thing about pizza is getting together with the "angels" you love and let everyone make up their own unique pizza.

Ingredients for the dough:
2 cups flour
½ cup warm water
½ cup Pellegrino water
2 teaspoons yeast
3 tablespoons olive oil
1 tablespoon sugar
2 teaspoons kosher salt
½ cup corn flour

Directions:
Mix the yeast and sugar in warm water and set aside.

Put 2 cups of all-purpose flour into a food processor with the salt. Mix and add 3 tablespoons of olive oil.

With mixer still running, add yeast mixture, then Pellegrino and let blend until the dough forms.

Remove and knead until smooth over lightly floured counter, about one minute. If dough is too sticky, add flour one tablespoon at a time to achieve desired consistency. If it is too dry, add one tablespoon at a time.

Separate dough into two balls, lightly coat with olive oil and wrap with plastic wrap. Refrigerate for at least 2 hours, preferably overnight.

You can also freeze dough balls for later use (recommend using airtight freezer bag for long term storage).

2 hours before using, remove plastic wrap and place dough in an oiled bowl, cover with plastic wrap and let it rise in a warm, draft free area.

When preparing pizza dough, sprinkle flour on a hard surface and knead dough into a circular shape. A rolling pin may also be used. If you are feeling adventurous you can try tossing your dough by first spreading it over the knuckles of your clenched fist. Then push it into the air with a twist of your wrist, and let it land back on your fist. With each toss the dough should spin and relax into a slightly larger shape, eventually requiring both fists to manipulate the dough.

Ingredients for the pizza:
1 ball of pizza dough, kneaded and rolled (see above)
½ cup corn flour
2 tablespoons olive oil
1 cup marinara sauce (see recipe)
½ lb fresh grated mozzarella cheese
1 lb cherry tomatoes sliced
6 leaves of fresh basil sliced

Directions for the pizza:
Turn your grill on to high heat and place the pizza stone directly on top of the grill. Adjust the flames so that they do not touch the bottom of the pizza stone. Close the grill lid and allow the stone to heat up for at least 20 minutes.

When you are ready to make your pizza, liberally sprinkle corn flour over your pizza peel or baking sheet before rolling it out. This will prevent the pizza from sticking to the pan.

Once the dough is rolled out on the pizza peel and before adding any ingredients, lightly brush the surface of the dough with olive oil. This will allow the dough to cook evenly and create a crispy, golden-brown crust.

Gently spread the marinara sauce over the dough leaving about ½ inch of the outside rim of the dough exposed.

Generously cover the sauce with the grated cheese.

Spread the tomato slices and basil evenly over the cheese.

Once you have your pizza creation ready, gently slide the pizza on the pizza stone by holding the peel at an angle and gently shaking it back and forth. You may want to have a spatula handy to help guide the pizza on to the stone.

Cover the grill and bake for 10-15 minutes, checking at least every 5 minutes to make sure the pizza is not burning. You can use your spatula to gently lift the edge of the pizza and check the bottom of the crust. The pizza is done when the bottom of the crust is a light golden brown and the cheese is fully melted.

Using the pizza peel, remove the pizza and let cool at room temperature for 5-10 minutes before serving.

RECIPE #6:

IF YOU CAN'T STAND THE HEAT, GET OUT OF THE KITCHEN

The Essential Ingredient:
Be loyal

Life is a lot like cooking. You get to pick your ingredients and create your own dish. But it is not as easy as it sounds. You don't get to wake up one day and declare yourself the head chef in charge of all things important in your life. You have to work your way to that position, and along the way you will spend a lot of time standing in someone else's kitchen; following their recipes. The key is to use these opportunities to learn as much as you can, and always respect that it is their kitchen not yours. There is an old saying, "if you can't stand the heat, you need to get out of the kitchen." If you cannot be loyal to someone else's recipes, you need to find another kitchen.

After graduating college, the Air Force sent me to Officers Training School at Lackland Air Force Base in Texas. This was an entirely different experience from basic training. While basic training was designed to break down enlisted people and build them back as a team, officers training focused on individual achievement. In basic training, we had to complete our final physical fitness test as a team. The last event was a 1.5-mile run that had to be completed within a certain time. When one of our classmates fell out due to exhaustion, a group of us stopped and picked him up, carrying him the rest of the way; otherwise, none of us would have graduated. In contrast, at officer's training school, you ran as an individual. I actually saw people fall down during the 1.5-mile run and others simply jumped over them to get by. It was every person for themselves.

It is interesting to note that there was very little about Officers Training School that resembled the real Air Force. I had already been through basic training and served seven years as an enlisted person, so I understood and appreciated the need to develop young people and instill discipline, while weeding out those who would not likely survive the military way of life. I also worked for officers who treated their enlisted personnel with tremendous respect, but this environment was almost brutal in its attempt to drive people to their breaking point. If the instructors thought you were incapable of making it through the program, they would do everything they could to get you to voluntarily withdraw from it. They called it Self-Initiated Elimination (SIE).

One of these candidates was my roommate. His name was Billy and he was one of the most remarkable young men I have ever met. Billy had gone through Navy ROTC in college with the hope of becoming a naval aviator. After his junior year, he found out he was not going to get a pilot training slot. He was so determined to be a military pilot, that he quit college and joined the Marines. While in the Marines, Billy finished college and applied for Officers Candidate School and their prestigious pilot's training program. He was accepted, only to discover he had a medical condition that prevented him from being a pilot. But he did not give up. After he got out of the Marines, Billy managed to clear his medical condition and qualify to join the Air Force Pilots Training Program. He went through preliminary flight training and finished at the top of his class. Afterwards, they sent him to Officers Training School, where he became my roommate.

Billy was extremely bright and was in the best physical condition of anyone I had ever met before or since. More importantly, he had a real passion for military aviation. It was all he ever talked about. After all of those years in ROTC and the Marines, he was in incredible shape. The minimum score to pass the physical fitness test at Officers Training School was 200 points on a 750-point scale. Most of us barely passed the first time, but Billy scored the maximum 750 points.

The academic regimen at Officers Training School was not very difficult. Most of it involved rote memorization of the different regulations and rules of military procedure. I remember the night before our first academic test, Billy and I studied for hours to the point we could recite the material backwards and forwards. The next day, our class was taken to a room where the test was administered. There was no instructor in the room, but there was a small window in the door, and every now and then an instructor would peek through the window to observe us. I was almost done with the test when two instructors burst into the room and grabbed Billy by both arms, literally dragging him out. We were all stunned. When I finished my test and returned to our dorm room, there was a note on my pillow from Billy telling me that he was forced to "SIE" because he was accused of looking over my shoulder during the test. This did not make any sense to me because Billy knew the material as well as I did. There was no reason for him to cheat.

Billy had been removed from our barracks and placed in administrative detention. I found out where they were keeping him and went to visit him. Billy looked me in the eye and told me that he did not do it, but the instructors gave him no choice but to resign. You cannot imagine the disappointment and angst in this young man's eyes.

I went to see the officers in charge of our barracks to appeal on Billy's behalf, but they would not budge from their position. I knew in my heart that they were wrong, yet there was nothing that I could do about it.

Billy's removal from the program had a terrible impact on the morale of our group. Having already served on active duty, I kept trying to reassure my classmates that the "real" Air Force was nothing like this environment; however, it is hard to explain this to a young person fresh out of college who already thinks they have made the biggest mistake of their life. Over the next several months, 25 percent of our class elected to SIE.

There were a lot of lessons I learned during this period. The first and most difficult lesson of all is that sometimes life is just not fair. There will be times in your life when you will suffer at the hands of others. But I also learned that even though bad things will happen, it is up to you to decide what to do with these experiences. You don't always get to choose what happens in your life, but you do get to decide how you want to deal with the outcome. You can learn and grow or you can be angry and make excuses. It is ultimately your choice.

Over the years, I have developed an almost fatalist attitude about these periods in my life. When confronted with challenging periods I simply can't control, I live by the solemn belief that if you work hard and do the right things for the right reasons, life will take care of itself. Either you will succeed in that environment, or God will put you somewhere else. You gain nothing by sweating over what you cannot control. This lesson became even more important when I finished OTS and got back to the "real" Air Force.

A week after pinning on my bars as a second lieutenant, I was assigned to the Air Force Systems Command at Eglin Air Force Base in Florida; here I was assigned to work on the development of a new state-of-the-art air-to-air missile. Six months later, command sent down a new general to take over the program. Our new boss had a reputation as being "hell on wheels." His name was General Charles E. Franklin; he spoke with a deep southern drawl and loved to use backcountry anachronisms, leading the casual observer to think he was not very sophisticated. It did not take you long to realize he had a razor sharp memory and a command of information well beyond anyone I have ever met before or since. Gen. Franklin was tough, but fair. He demanded a lot from us, but he gave us much more in return.

The truth is, he "fired" me after his first week on the job. As it turned out, I had been assigned a position that was previously held by a much more senior officer. When the general showed up on station and asked to meet his section chiefs, he found me in one of these positions. Without even meeting me, he immediately replaced me with a much more senior person.

I was not going to go away quietly. I had already been working in that position for more than five months and I was just starting to build a good team. That next morning, I went to his office, closed the door, and asked to speak to him one-on-one. I told him flatly that I did not think he was making the right decision. I went on to tell him that although I was just a second lieutenant, I had been in the Air Force for more than seven years and knew I could do the job. I then apologized for my abruptness, but I wanted him to know how strongly I felt.

The general sat back in his chair, looked me square in the eyes, and proceeded to teach me a very important lesson. I like to call it the true definition of loyalty.

According to General Franklin, the greatest form of loyalty is to question your boss when you think he is wrong. He even went as far as saying that it was your absolute duty to do so. But do it privately, he said, and once the discussion is over, whether you agree or not, carry out the decision as though it was your own. If you cannot do that in good conscience, then you should not be working for that person. If they cannot accept your honesty, they do not deserve to have you working for them.

He went on to say that this is not only the true definition of loyalty, but also the cornerstone of good leadership. Too many "leaders" disagree with their boss' direction, but rather than challenge their boss, they pass down the direction with comments like, "I know the old man is off his rocker, but we have to do this anyway." Weaker leaders do this, thinking they are somehow avoiding the responsibility for a bad decision. The truth is, when they take this approach, their subordinates no longer see them as leaders. They see them as order takers, who simply pass along the bad news. On the other hand, if a leader embraces the boss' direction and delivers it to his team with full conviction, the team may still not like it, but in the end, they will respect his or her leadership. More importantly, they will likely achieve the organization's objectives with much greater success.

The general also cautioned that loyalty couldn't be blind to injustice. That is why he said you should not be working for someone if they ever ask you to do anything that compromises your integrity.

When we finished our discussion, he gave me back my job, but also gave me this warning: "I will treat you like the position you are filling, not the one you think you have earned. If you cannot meet my expectations, I will fire you on the spot." He went on to say, "If you cannot handle this, don't let the door hit you on the way out."

It was his way of saying, "If you can't stand the heat, get out of the kitchen."

I spent the next four years trying to prove to him that I was the right person for the job, only to realize that he was right all along. You see, Gen. Franklin turned out to be another one of those "angels" in my life who saw more in me than I did. He knew that he could challenge me to be a better officer and a better person. He set the bar high and each time I reached it, he would raise it even higher. While I worked for him, I was selected officer of the year twice and earned several medals for distinguished service; but the greatest honor I ever received in my military service came on the day I finished my last day of duty. At my going away party, Gen. Franklin stood up and told the story about how we met, including how I marched into his office and told him he was wrong. Then he thanked me for having the courage to say so and the loyalty to never mention it again.

I have carried that form of loyalty to every person I have worked for, and I have tried to teach it to every leader who has worked for me. I learned that my best contribution to my superior is to make their decisions succeed. Fortunately, I have never worked for someone who tried to compromise my integrity, but I have on occasion carried the burden of an assignment I did not fully agree with. I was always comforted in the fact that I gave them my best advice, and they chose this course of action in spite of my best efforts to convince them otherwise. That is the boss' prerogative, as well as the subordinate's duty.

I also learned from Gen. Franklin that you must have an open mind even after you make a decision. He could have stuck to his guns and dismissed me on the spot. Instead, he listened and used it as an opportunity to teach and develop a young officer. He also understood that success does not come from being "right" all of the time; it comes from making the right decision when it matters most. I believe Mark Twain said it best when he wrote, "It is not what you don't know that gets you in trouble; it is what you think you know that just ain't so."

If you really want to be successful, the workplace is not the only place where loyalty is required. In fact, it is even more important in other facets of your life. The level of your loyalty you apply will directly correlate to the level of success you will achieve in your faith, as well as in the relationships with your family and friends.

Just remember, as Gen. Franklin taught me, loyalty is a two-way street. In order for it to be effective, it must be based on certain moral tenets such as mutual trust and respect. Loyalty, without a strong moral basis, will often lead to resentment, and ultimately, betrayal. Over the years, I have counseled many friends who felt betrayed by someone else. I usually ask them the same question: "What did you do to earn their loyalty?"

When confronted with disloyalty, ask yourself these questions: Did you respect them? Did you try to understand their differences? Would you have placed their interests before your own? Would they have ever considered you as one of their "angels?" The most difficult, yet important question you have to ask yourself is whether or not you were loyal to them. If you cannot affirmatively answer these questions with honesty and conviction, then maybe you did not deserve their loyalty in the first place.

If you agree that life is a lot like cooking, then you will also agree that kitchens are the places in life where we learn how to cook. Some of these kitchens will teach you good things, yet others will teach you what not to do. If you have a good moral compass, work hard and do the right things, you will be able to use all of these lessons to create your recipe for success.

Risotto with Porcini Mushrooms

*I can't think of any dish that requires more **loyalty and hard work** than risotto. Risotto is a uniquely Italian dish of rice cooked in broth to a creamy consistency. The broth may be meat-based, fish-based, or vegetable-based. Most risottos include some type of cheese, butter, and onion. It is one of the most common ways of cooking rice in Italy.*

It is best to use a high-starch, short-grain to make risotto. These rice have the ability to absorb liquids and to release starch and are therefore stickier than long grain varieties. There are several varieties, but I prefer a good quality Arborio.

The rice is first cooked at relatively high heat in a sauté of onion and olive oil to coat each grain in a light film of fat. This is called toasting, and the objective is to toast the rice until you see a dark spot start to form at the center of each rice kernel. The next step is to add white or red wine and allow it to be fully absorbed by the grains. Finally, a very hot stock is gradually added in small amounts while stirring gently, almost constantly. The stirring is the most important step because it loosens the starch molecules from the outside of the rice grains into the surrounding liquid, creating a smooth creamy-textured liquid. At the very end you add butter and finely grated Parmigiano-Reggiano cheese to create a creamy and smooth texture.

Properly cooked risotto is rich and creamy but still with some resistance or bite (al dente). If you prefer a healthier version, you can cut back on the cheese, in fact I sometimes make my risotto without any cheese at all.

Ingredients:

1 cup dried porcini mushrooms
½ onion, chopped
3 celery sticks, diced
2 tablespoons Italian parsley, minced
1 ½ cups Arborio rice
½ cup white wine
2 cups chicken broth
3 handfuls freshly grated Parmesan cheese
¼ stick butter
2 tablespoons olive oil
Salt & pepper

Directions:

In a pot on medium heat, simmer dried porcini mushrooms in chicken stock for 20 minutes. Drain mushrooms and reserve broth for later use.

In a pre-heated pan on high heat, add olive oil. Then add onion, celery, salt & pepper. Cook until vegetables are softened (about 4-5 minutes). Mix mushroom into onions. Cook 3-5 minutes.

Stir in 1-½ cups of Arborio rice. Continue stirring until rice toasts. When rice is properly toasted, you will notice a golden brown spot start to form in each rice kernel. This will take at least 10 minutes.

Add ½ cup white wine and cook until reduced (about 3 minutes).

Ladle in enough chicken broth to barely cover the rice. Cover and cook for 20-30 minutes, stirring occasionally. Keep adding more broth and stirring until rice is firm but ready to eat.

Uncover and mix in butter, parsley, and grated Parmesan cheese. Turn off heat and let sit for 3-5 minutes before serving.

RECIPE #7:

SOMETIMES YOU HAVE TO CHANGE THE RECIPE

The Essential Ingredient:
Get paid doing what you enjoy

I have always been torn between the concepts of destiny and fate. Is our life a recipe of pre-ordained events over which we have no control or is our destiny a random path dictated by the choices we make? There are those things we can control and certainly a great many things we cannot. I would like to believe that the only things "pre-ordained" in our life are where we begin and the fact that one day we will pass on from this earth. The path we lead and the decisions we make will determine our fate. Intermingled along the way will be a series of challenges and opportunities we may or may not be able to control; we can choose how we respond to them, learn from them, and ultimately decide our own fate.

Sometimes these decisions lead us in the right direction, but there will be times when we find ourselves lost and far from where we thought we were headed. When this happens, it is very important to know your recipe for success based on your goals, values and God-given talents. Your goals will tell you where you are going, your values are the moral compass to guide you through life's challenges, and your God-given talents will transport you to your destination.

It is equally important to understand that recipes should never be written in stone. Your recipe should be a living, breathing document that will grow with your life experiences. There will be times in your life when it will be necessary to change your recipe.

My mother died of cancer at the relatively young age of 62. I realize she had no control over this horrible disease, but I also know that the stress in her life lead her to alcoholism, which led to obesity, and eventually she became susceptible to a disease that claimed her life. Who knows what would have happened under different circumstances, and maybe it was her fate to die of cancer; but what is really important is everything that happened in between. Accepting those challenges as they arise, charting a new path, setting new goals, and building a better place in life is what matters.

For instance, I never planned to make the Air Force a career. I only joined to get an education and move on with my life. I did get a great education, but in ways I never would have imagined. I learned a whole new set of values — honor, duty, loyalty, and teamwork. This experience had a profound impact on my life and forever changed me. I loved the military and was very good at it. I thought for certain this would be my career, but a series of events beyond my control changed everything.

I was coming up on a new promotion and my commander told me they were considering me for a prestigious assignment to the Pentagon. I was so excited that I could not wait to tell Karen about our new adventure. When I got home and told her, she gave me a soft, yet somewhat subdued smile, and said, "I'm so proud of you, but there is something I have to tell you." At that point, the tears started rolling down her cheeks.

Several months earlier, Karen lost her brother Keith in a tragic diving accident. Of her four brothers, Keith was the closest to her in both age and affection, and he was one of my closest friends. The pain of losing Keith was overwhelming to the entire family, but the emotional toil on her parents was simply devastating. Losing a loved one is painful enough, but losing a child is beyond comprehension. This is something that no parent should ever have to endure.

The day I came home to tell her about our new assignment, she had received a call from her family. The stress of losing Keith had caused her father's health to fail and they could not handle running the family business anymore. They wanted her to come home and take it over. This would mean I would have to resign my commission from the Air Force and move our family back to Cocoa

Beach.

There really was no choice in this matter. Family comes first and Karen had always put my career ahead of her own. Years before, she had quit college so that she could put me through school and raise our children. She made so many sacrifices along the way and I knew that it was my time to make sacrifices for her, but I must admit that regardless of how necessary and important this decision was, resigning from the Air Force was not very easy for me to accept. I had finally found something I enjoyed and was good at, but I knew in my heart that it was time to change the recipe for our lives.

So we moved back to Cocoa Beach, where I immediately found a job with the new commercial space program that had just started up at Cape Canaveral Air Force Station.

At first, I was very excited about this new opportunity. I was part of a team that would build and operate the first commercial space launch facility in the United States. We took one of the old, rusted out Mercury-era launch pads and rebuilt it into a brand-new commercial launch facility. Once the pad was built, we constructed and launched 12 Atlas-Centaur rockets into space with a variety of commercial payloads. I became the pneumatics and propulsion engineer for the program and sat on the launch panel for most of these launches. I can honestly say that I was a rocket scientist.

It may surprise you to know that being a "rocket scientist" is not all that it is cracked up to be. The work was not nearly as challenging and glamorous as you might expect, and in many ways, it reminded me of working on an oil derrick. The American public would be surprised to know how woefully antiquated and obsolete our space program technology has become. Most of the equipment we used on the launch pad was designed and built in the 1950's. Think about this for one moment — the most advanced spacecraft in the world is the Space Shuttle, and it was deployed before the first personal computer ever hit the market. Most of our current functional space technology is scientifically inferior to the latest cell phones.

To make matters worse, like most government facilities, there was an army of bureaucrats you had to wade through in order to get anything done. Since many of the engineers came from the era before personal computers and did not know how to use them, all of the paperwork had to be hand-written. We were supposed to be a "commercial" launch facility, yet we were being asphyxiated in a sea of red tape and bureaucracy. We did manage to launch 12 rockets, but we put three of those rockets in the ocean with over $180 million worth of satellites still attached.

I became disillusioned with the path I was on. I started to hate my job and grew more and more frustrated each day. This new recipe was simply not working for me, and my attitude was starting to affect my relationship with Karen. Looking back, I think that somewhere deep inside I probably resented her for taking me out of my "successful" Air Force career.

But this new experience was working for Karen. She was a phenomenal success in her new career and she completely revitalized the family business. This allowed her parents to take the time they needed to heal. They even bought a new motor home and started traveling around the country. I was very proud of her, and I knew in my heart we had made the right decision. I also knew I had to find a way to make something positive out of this experience before I caused irreparable damage to our relationship.

There will be times in your life where things do not turn out the way you planned. Be it a personal tragedy, a life changing event, or a change in direction of your career, there will be forks in the road that cause you to pause and reconsider the direction you are headed. The one thing these critical moments share in common is they force you to stop and think about what is truly important in your life. It is during these times when it is essential to have your own personal recipe for success. You have to set meaningful goals for your life, build a solid system of values and appreciate your God-given talents. Without a basic recipe or a roadmap to guide you through life's many challenges, you may not realize just how lost you really are.

This period of my life was a wake-up call. I had to embrace

the fact that we were doing the best for our family. I had to accept that my career needed to take a back seat to a much more important agenda – raising our children. Looking back, I can honestly say that this was one of the most important periods in our lives.

The one advantage of working in the space industry is that we started our workday very early and finished before the children got out of school. I would get off work every day early enough to pick them up directly from school, take them to the park, and still make it home in time to make dinner before Karen got home from work.

It was during this time that I really started learning how to cook. I would cook almost every night and we would sit down and eat together as a family, sharing the stories of our day. I cannot stress how important these times were to the success of our family. Too many families do not take the time to do something so simple as eat together or, if they do, it is in front of a television.

The most important lesson I gained from this experience is that, when it comes to children, there is no adequate substitute for time. I have heard too many people say, "spending quality time with your children is more important than quantity time." I have learned this is a lie we tell ourselves to soothe our guilty feelings for not spending enough time with our families. In order to appreciate the importance of time to children, you first must understand that children have a different perspective on time than adults.

Let me give you a simple analogy to illustrate this point.

You have probably noticed that as we grow older, the years fly by faster and faster. This is not because time changes as we get older, but because our perspective of time changes as we age. For instance, to an adult, a year is only a small percentage of their life; whereas to a child, a year is a significant part of their life. Just imagine the feeling of standing on the 2nd floor balcony of a skyscraper and looking down, then going to the 50th floor and looking down. The difference in what you feel is simply your perspective based on where you were before.

So when you postpone doing something with your child, to you it may be only a few hours, days or weeks; but from a child's perspective, it is an eternity. Just watch a child's impatient face when you tell them that Christmas is still two weeks away. Yet in the back of your mind, you are wondering where you will find the time to get everything done. The fact is, our children need both quantity and quality time.

The best part of this period in my life was getting to spend so much time with our children, Cara and Brian. Hence, I was able to coach almost every team they played on since they were old enough to play team sports. I also discovered that I had a real passion for coaching and working with young people. I like to tell people that if children were born at 6 years of age and never got older than 12, I'd have a hundred children.

Later in life, as my professional career took off, coaching their teams became a real challenge for my busy schedule; yet I chose to continue coaching all of my children's teams because I knew how important it was to them for me to be there. As a parent sitting in the bleachers, it would be too easy to show up late, which sometimes becomes "not at all." I knew that the most important ingredient to the success of my family was making the commitment to spend as much time with them as possible.

I think the first time that I really understood how important this time was for our family came years later when we went to visit Brian in college. It is also one of my proudest moments as a parent.

We had planned to take Brian away for the weekend, but he told us he had a commitment that he could not get out of - he was coaching a youth basketball team at a local church. I will never forget sitting in those stands watching him coach these young boys. He was good at it and you could tell that these boys really liked and respected him. But the best compliment came from one of the parents sitting next to us in the bleacher. When they found out we were Brian's parents, they told us what a difference Brian had made in their son's life. Their son had no interest in sports and was not getting along with the children in school, but since Brian started coaching him his whole attitude changed. They said he was happier than ever and had discovered a real passion for sports. They then asked us what Brian did for a living, and even asked if he was a schoolteacher. You should have seen the surprise on their faces when we told them that he was a sophomore in college. I knew, at that moment, that all of those years we spent together on the ball fields and basketball courts had paid off.

During these years, I had the opportunity to coach hundreds of children across many sports and levels of competition. I wish all children were good children, but I can tell you I have yet to meet a "bad" one that did not get there without influence from his or her parents. I know this idea will inflame some people's sensitivities, but I believe that with children, like most of the really important things in our lives, you literally reap what you sow. If you want your children to grow up to be mentally healthy and responsible adults, you must lead by example. You must hold them accountable, give them love and respect, and make sure you are there when they need you most.

Interestingly enough, the most "successful" children I have met were heavily involved in extracurricular activities, be it sports, music, or church and club-related activities. In fact, studies have shown that children who participate in extracurricular activities achieve a full grade point higher in their average grades than children who don't participate. If you want your children to be successful, you have to invest your time in them. The good news is - the rewards are endless.

This was definitely the best investment we ever made in our family. Cara and Brian have grown into amazing adults who are extremely successful in both their careers and personal lives. Karen and I are honored when people meet them and invariably tell us what great children we have raised. The irony is if you ask them about their favorite memories as a child, they will point back to that same period of time when I was disappointed with how my career had turned out. What I had perceived to be a sacrifice was in actuality a wonderful gift.

In retrospect, even my career was enhanced during this period. When I left active duty, I immediately joined the Air Force

Reserves where I was assigned to a small team that specialized in organizational re-engineering. The Air Force was using this team to teach commercial business practices to operational units. Base commanders were now called "CEO's" and finance directors became "CFO's", but none of them really understood what it meant to operate like a business. Our job was to use our combined military and commercial experience to bridge the gap between industry and the military skillsets. My team consisted of several PhD's, attorneys and business leaders, most of whom outranked me. None of them wanted the hassle and paperwork of leading the team, so by my second year they "elected" me the team leader. Our team won the Air Force Reserves Project of the Year Award eight consecutive years in a row. This experience kept me connected with a profession I truly enjoyed — the Air Force.

As I said before, not everything works out the way you plan, and sometimes you have to take a step back to move in the right direction. There may be setbacks and distractions along the way that will make it difficult to achieve your goals, but the key is to never allow yourself to lose sight of what is really important. If you must, take a step back and use the time wisely to invest in yourself and your family.

I recall when I first enlisted in the service, there was a large group of us that went through basic training, technical training, and on to our first assignment together. We all shared a similar dream to use the Air Force to get as much education as possible, save some money, and go off to college. But when we got our first assignment, most of my friends got caught up in their social lives and never did the things they needed to achieve their dreams. At the end of their four years of duty, they really did not have much more than what they started with.

I was determined to not let this phase of my life derail my goals. I used every chance to learn more and take on more responsibilities at work. I talked my company into letting me introduce the commercial launch team to the personal computer. We created the first automated scheduling program for the commercial space program; this allowed all of the engineering disciplines to effectively coordinate their efforts, therefore cutting months off of the launch vehicle processing time. We also automated all of our launch system procedures to expedite the approval process. It was so successful that the military adopted our program to manage the ongoing development of the Eastern Test Range that supports the launch industry. Of course, the company that held the contract needed an expert in this new system, so one day I got a call asking me to join their team and oversee their project management team.

My professional career was on the upswing again, and our family life could not have been better. We bought our "dream home," our children were performing great in school, and life was pretty good. During this same time at work, I was promoted three times and, at age 36, became the youngest senior manager in our division.

I had just received that front-row office overlooking the ocean with my own personal secretary. Life was good, but there was still something missing. It took a truly good friend to help me realize it.

The day after I received my promotion, one of my friends stopped by to see me. He had been a senior engineer with the company for many years and held some very lucrative patents. He really did not need to work for a living, so he had the freedom to speak candidly. He sat down and said, "Congratulations on your promotion. What are you going to do now?" He pointed out that the youngest vice president in the company was 52 years old. I had been promoted three times in the past year and somehow he knew that I was not going to be satisfied sitting at that desk for the next 15 years. From anyone else in the organization, I would have taken this as jealousy, but in my heart I knew he was right. As it turned out, he was one of those "angels" in my life who saw something much greater in me. A few weeks later, with his words still ringing in my ears, I made a decision to completely change my career.

Looking back, I realized I had learned to adjust to this situation, and if not for the intervention of others, I might still be living in Cocoa Beach working at the Cape. Not that there is anything wrong with that, but my life became much more fulfilling since I changed my direction. The truth is, I became an aerospace engineer because the Air Force made it a condition of my scholarship, and I ended up in the space industry when I followed my wife back to her hometown. It was never my dream to go down that path, but as it turned out, I was very good at it.

This is another important ingredient that became part of the recipe of my life — do not stick with something just because you are good or successful at it. You need to find something in life that will stimulate your passion and challenge you to meet your potential. Otherwise, you will never be happy or satisfied.

This is certainly not a new idea. It is a philosophy that predates modern civilization. Confucius was a Chinese thinker and social philosopher who lived five centuries before Christ. His teachings and philosophy have deeply influenced Asian thought and life. In his teachings, Confucius says, "Real success is finding your lifework in the work that you love."

Throughout my life, I have met many people who would be considered "successful." I have met captains of industry, professional athletes, celebrities, politicians, and heads of state. But once you get to know these people from a personal standpoint, you quickly discover that while they may be successful at their chosen profession, some of them have personal lives that are a complete wreck. That is why I believe it is important to make sure your definition of success and the goals you set out to achieve are the ones that will truly make you happy. Being good at something is not the only thing to consider; it is only one of many things to consider.

I have discovered that success can be grouped into three areas: professional, personal, and spiritual. Your true happiness depends on how hard you want to work at each area of your life and what sacrifices and compromises you are willing to make. For instance, you can be successful at work, but it may come at a cost to your success at home with your family. I have learned that the most successful and happy people I know have found a way to maintain a proper balance across all areas of their lives.

I have also learned that true professional success means getting paid for doing what you enjoy. Probably the only really bad advice my mother ever gave me was to find a job that would pay me enough to do what I want to do during the other 16 hours of the day I wasn't working. Her generation treated their jobs as a means to an end. It took many years traveling down different paths to look back and realize that her generation was wrong.

True success is defined on your own terms, based on your abilities, and the level of effort you want to put into it. Simply stated, find what you enjoy doing and be the best you can at it. That is why I believe it is important for each person to sit down and reflect on where they have been and where they are going, access the talents that God has given them, and ask the really hard question my friend asked me, "Is this really what you want?"

As you can see by now, my life was never a course that I chartered. Yes, I had broad dreams of getting an education and being "successful," but it took many years to understand what success meant to me in my life. I had to realize that what really made me happy was having a wonderful and loving family, a strong relationship with God, and a profession in which I could make a difference in the lives of others. However, I also wanted to make the kind of money that would allow me to do things my parents could never do — travel the world, build a beautiful home, and put my children through college. Eventually my path led me to a place where I actually got paid doing what I enjoy most.

This is extremely important in deciding your professional life. I have had a great many jobs and I was pretty good at most of them. But in most cases, I never really had a true passion for what I was doing. I didn't wake up in the morning and say; "I can't wait to get in the office today!" My greatest professional successes came when I was doing something that stimulated my passion to the point that it really did not feel like work to me at all.

You should also approach your educational goals from the same perspective. Gaining a good education is much more than something to add to your resume. Too often I have met people who pursued a degree in something they thought would get them a great job, without considering what they really wanted in a profession. It is much more important to pick a degree program that truly interests you and stimulates your passion to learn. You will discover that the true value of an education is not just the accumulation of knowledge, but learning how to think from a different perspective. With few obvious exceptions, your major in college does not always determine your future profession.

I have spoken to groups all over the country on leadership and job performance, and the one thing I tell aspiring leaders that you cannot teach is passion. You can fan the flames, but the spark has to be there. Any reasonably intelligent person can be trained to perform almost any routine task, but if they do not have a passion for what they do, they will never be completely satisfied or successful.

The key to building great organizations is finding people capable of being passionate about their work, then creating the right environment for them to succeed. Given the right tools, training, and leadership, a passionate person can accomplish almost anything. I would also go so far as to say that if you have given someone all of these things and they still are not succeeding, then you have a responsibility to both the individual and your organization to help them move on to a new career someplace else. Hopefully they will find a place that kindles their true passion in life.

Also, you are not helping yourself by staying with something just because the pay may be good or simply because you are good at it. Life is too short to spend most of your waking hours doing something you do not really care about. Sooner or later it will impact your performance, as well as the other important areas of your life. It is also much better to change your recipe before someone else does it for you.

It is important to have a recipe for your life, but you must realize that sometimes you have to change the recipe. No one has a crystal ball that will foresee where life will take us. As long as you have the right ingredients, such as faith, family and friends, you will find your recipe for success.

The best Coq au Vin I ever had

I used to think I made a great Coq au Vin. It was one of my favorite dishes, so I studied all of the traditional recipes and worked diligently to produce what I believed was a very good Coq Au Vin. I even created a white-wine version with garlic and lemon that I call Coq Au Vin Blanc (see recipe at the end of the book). I was so enamored with my Coq au Vin that I would not even order this dish off the menu of any restaurant that we visited lest I be disappointed with their version. But one day I was dining at a new French restaurant, and they had Coq au Vin on the menu. The waiter promised me that it would be the best Coq au Vin I would ever have. He was so insistent that I gave in and ordered the Coq au Vin.

It was quite simply the best Coq au Vin I ever had! I was so impressed that I asked to speak to the chef and ask him how me made this fantastic dish. When he came to the table, he explained that this was an old family recipe that was handed down from generation to generation. He then proceeded to break down the recipe in steps for me, some of which did not make any sense (marinating the pancetta and coating the flour-covered chicken with tomato paste to name a few). Nonetheless, he was very clear that you must follow each step and use every ingredient exactly as stated.

When I got home from that trip, the first thing I did was run to the store and buy a good roaster chicken and a large bottle of Burgundy wine (yes, he was adamant that you have to use Burgundy wine). I made his version of Coq au Vin, and I have to admit it was still the best Coq au Vin I have ever tasted. At that point I knew - ***it was time to change the recipe!***

So here is the recipe for the best Coq au Vin I have ever had, and it is a tribute to the amazing chef who taught me how to make it – Eric Cousin. I have also included my original recipe for Coq au Vin at the back of the book, just in case you want to compare the two. But trust me, this one is better.

Ingredients:
Whole chicken, cut in pieces
1 lb carrots diced
8 oz pearl onions
1 gallon Burgundy wine
8 oz bottom mushroom quartered
1 lb small fingerling potatoes peeled
8 oz pancetta, chopped
4 oz tomato paste
½ cup all purpose flour
12 oz chicken stock
4-6 tablespoons olive oil
15 oz potato, turned blanched
3 oz parsley, freshly minced
Salt & Black Pepper

For the bouquet garni:
4 oz fresh thyme
4 bay leaves dried
¼ oz whole black pepper corn

Directions:
Prepare the bouquet garni by wrapping the thyme, bay leaves and peppercorns in cheese cloth.

In a large bowl or heavy plastic bag, combine all chicken parts, carrots, onions, mushrooms and the pancetta. Pour in the Burgundy wine and add the bouquet garni. Refrigerate and allow to marinate for 36 to 48 hours.

Preheat oven to 375 degrees.

Use a colander to separate the chicken and the vegetables from the wine marinade. Reserve balance of the marinade in a saucepan.

Place the saucepan on high heat and bring the marinade to a boil. Gently skim all of the foam off the surface of the marinade, then reduce the heat to medium and cook until slightly thickened (about 10 minutes).

In a preheated pan on high heat, add 2-3 tablespoons of olive oil and evenly brown the chicken on all sides. Set aside to cool.

Coat the chicken with flour, and then use a rubber spatula to heavily coat the flour-covered chicken with tomato paste.

Pour the reduced marinade into a Dutch oven with the reserved vegetables, pancetta and the bouquet garni. Place the chicken in the Dutch oven and add wine as necessary to completely cover the chicken. Add about one teaspoon each of salt and pepper.

Cover the Dutch oven and bake at 375 degrees for 1 hour, checking occasionally.

Prepare the potatoes rissole style by first placing them in boiling water for 10 minutes. Remove and drain off an excess liquid.

In a preheated pan on high heat, add 2 tablespoons olive oil and sauté the potatoes until golden brown. Salt and pepper to taste.

When chicken is ready, garnish with fresh chopped parsley and serve with the rissole potato and the vegetables from the pot.

RECIPE #8:

RECIPES TO WORK WITH

The Essential Ingredient:
Be true to your values and value others

I often think about that summer day in 1975, eating lunch off the back of a station wagon on the side of a dusty Nebraska highway, and resolving that one day I would be successful. At the time, I believed the only true scorecard for success was money. So I left home with nothing but the clothes on my back and made it my objective to obtain a good education, get a job, and make lots of money. But the closer I got to this "dream," I realized that it lacked substance. I may have been good at what I did, but I really had no passion for it. While there were many parts of my life that gave me immense satisfaction, such as my family, my work felt just like that — work. My definition of success had changed and I knew it was time to change the recipe.

That is why it is so important to clearly understand the most important ingredients of your personal success — your values, your goals, and your God-given talents. Dream big, but dream with a purpose these ingredients can support. Always remember that true success comes from a balance of your professional, personal, and spiritual lives.

About the same time we got married, Karen's uncle, David Siegel, started a resort timeshare company near Orlando, Fl. Over the next several years, he offered me many chances to join his company, but I never really took it seriously. The problem was, I had no desire to work for a relative, let alone in an industry completely removed from my education or experience. But as fate would have it, the last time David offered me a job just happened to be the day after my friend walked into my office to "congratulate" me on my new promotion.

David told me that he would give me a "PhD in business." He wanted me to be his assistant, follow him around, and take on whatever projects he needed done. We met several times over the next week, and I actually turned him down three times after he made his offer, which included less money than I was making at the time.

It was not about the money. The truth is that I was simply scared to leave my comfort zone. I accumulated seven years of college and invested 12 years of experience in my previous profession. I was very good at it, but in my heart, knew something was missing. That "something" was true passion for my work. I needed an opportunity to achieve my potential, and he was willing to give me that opportunity.

So I took the job.

At the time I joined David, he had developed several resorts in Central Florida, bought and sold land, and created a variety of business ventures. Prior to opening his first resort, he had already become a multi-millionaire back in the 1970's, when being a multi-millionaire actually meant something. David expanded his company into the resort timeshare business in 1983 when he opened Westgate Resorts just outside the "west gate" of Walt Disney World. By the time I joined him, he had about 2,200 employees and the company was doing quite well, with over several hundred million dollars in annual revenues.

Working for David was like going back to basic training. My "office" was an old desk in the back of a file room. He had me following him around from meeting to meeting in order to soak in as much as I could. Every night we would sit in his office until late in the evening, going over the business of the day.

Without a doubt, the best part about working for David was connecting with my inner passions. Although I was an engineer by education and experience, I was also an artist and musician by hobby. Above all, I really enjoy being in a place where I can make a positive difference in the lives of others. Working for David allowed me to bring all of these areas of my life together and create something very special. David was not only willing to teach me the business, but give me the latitude to be creative.

Within a few years, I worked my way out of the file room and started taking on more and more responsibility. Eventually, David made me his chief operating officer, and over the next several years, I was part of a team that built Westgate into one of the leaders in the destination resort industry, with 29 resorts across the country. Along the way, we have created just about every vacation theme you can dream up, from a historic colonial inn to a Western-style dude ranch, complete with a live rodeo and saloon. The best part is that we have also created incredible vacation memories for the millions of families that have visited our resorts.

The truth is, I gained as much from this experience as I was able to contribute. When David said he was going to give me a "PhD in business," what he really meant was that he was going to give me a "PhD" in his way of doing business that challenges anything I may have learned in business school.

One of the most important things I have learned from David is to never overlook a potential opportunity. With David, everything and everyone is a potential opportunity. There is an old saying, "Sometimes you have to kiss a lot of frogs to find a prince." David kisses every frog he meets. He is the most accessible billionaire you will ever meet. He answers every phone call, email, and letter that he receives. Keep in mind that he has more than 10,000 employees and 400,000 owners in his timeshare company alone. At times it can be unnerving. He will answer his cell phone during a meeting, in a movie theater, doctor's office, or airplane. I have even seen him answer his cell phone while he was giving a speech to more than 300 people. An opportunity rarely gets by David unnoticed.

Another important lesson I learned was to be hands on. There is a management theory called *Management by Walking Around*, but David believes that it does no good to be visible if you are not actively engaged in what is really going on in your business. Too often I see managers take the attitude of "don't sweat the small stuff." David knows that if you add up enough small stuff, it quickly becomes the big stuff. More importantly, if you train your people to pay attention to the little details, you can often prevent a small problem from growing into a bigger one. All you have to do is spend one day with the man, and you will gain a whole new appreciation for the little details that add up in your business. As he walks around his resorts, you will see him check the settings on the air conditioners and refrigerators in one of his many buildings. He wants every refrigerator set on the optimum setting for energy consumption because he knows he has more than 10,000 refrigerators out there, and if he can save $10 per month in electricity in each unit, that will result in substantial savings every year. He even reviews and signs every check before it goes out the door. Some people call it micro management. He calls it paying attention.

Finally, the greatest lesson I learned from David was to encourage criticism. He is a firm believer that too many businesses fail because their customers did not have the courage to tell them what they were doing wrong. When David is at someone else's place of business and he sees something out of sorts, he will always ask for the owner or manager to explain to him what he saw. There is nothing mean-spirited in his intent. David truly wants to help them get better. David, on the other hand, not only encourages criticism, he demands it. Whenever he interviews someone to manage one of his properties, he asks them to go spend a few days on the property and come back with a report of their observations. If they come back and say that everything looks great, he thanks them for their time and sends them on. But if they come in with a detailed list of what they saw that needed improvement, they are much more likely to get hired.

I would like to say that after all of these years working with David, I have successfully mastered all of the lessons he has taught me. However, like most great leaders, as soon as we get close, he raises the bar just a little bit higher. But I also believe that the day we stop learning is the day we stop living.

While working for David, I have had the opportunity to make a lot of money, travel the world, and meet many rich and famous people. I can also say that working with one of the richest men in

America is not an easy task. Like most successful entrepreneurs, his work is his hobby; therefore, the hours can be very long and the stress can sometimes be more than most people can handle. I was very fortunate I joined his team when our children were well past their adolescent years. I was also fortunate that I was already equipped with a strong work ethic, a sound moral compass, and most of all — a very supportive wife. I have witnessed firsthand what a high profile, high-pressure environment can do to individuals and their families.

In the corporate world, there will always be those individuals who value style over substance and seek to better themselves at the expense of others. I have always had a low tolerance for these types of people, sometimes even to my detriment. When I get frustrated with these challenges, I have to remind myself of something my mother used to tell me, "The cream always rises to the top."

Although it never seems to happen quickly enough, I have learned that if you hang around long enough, you will find that the universal law of "what goes around comes around" always vindicates those who do the right things and ultimately punishes those who don't. You truly do reap what you sow.

Over the years, I have acquired pretty good coping skill for dealing with these situations — work hard and always do the right thing for the right reason. If you do that and still get claimed by the injustice of those who do not, then God obviously needs you to be somewhere else.

But understand that "hard work" is more than just exerting effort. I have met a lot of people in the business world who appear to be very hard working and efficient, but under close examination, they are better at reporting results than actually achieving them. That is why it is important to understand the difference between being efficient and being effective. Efficient means doing things right, effective means doing the right things.

If you succeed in business, you will learn that the most valuable people in your organization are the ones who stand at the front line and represent your product. They stand at your assembly lines, answer your phones, and directly impact your customers. You need to support these people, help them succeed, and protect them from the back-office legions that think the reports they create are more important than the products you produce. As Colin Powell once said, "Shift the power and financial accountability to the folks who are bringing in the beans, not the ones who are counting or analyzing them."

I once read a great story that exemplifies the importance of recognizing the people that make a difference in your business:

During my second month of college, our professor gave us a pop quiz. I was a conscientious student and had breezed through the questions, until I read the last one: "What is the first name of the woman who cleans the school?

Surely this was some kind of joke. I had seen the cleaning woman several times. She was tall, dark-haired and in her 50s, but how would I know her name? I handed in my paper, leaving the last question blank.

Just before class ended, one student asked if the last question would count toward our quiz grade.

"Absolutely," said the professor. "In your careers, you will meet many people! All are significant. They deserve your attention and care, even if all you do is smile and say 'hello.'"

I've never forgotten that lesson. I also learned her name was Dorothy."

If professional success is important to you, then you really need to make sure you understand what it means to be successful in that environment. You need to understand what sacrifices will be expected and compare the potential reward to what it will cost the other areas of your life, both personal and spiritual.

This does not mean you cannot be successful in all areas of your life; you just have to be aware of the tradeoffs and compromises you will ultimately have to make. There is a parable in the Bible that says it is easier for a camel to pass through the eye of a needle than for a rich man to get into Heaven. Most people mistake that parable to mean it is literally impossible to balance a successful business and spiritual life. But what most people do not know is that in ancient times, most commerce was delivered by ox and camel, and a "needle" was the term used to describe an obstacle on a mountain trail where the camel driver had to train his camel to pass through on its hands and knees. It was very difficult to do, but not impossible.

I have learned that it is possible to achieve financial success without sacrificing personal and spiritual success. You just have to be willing to work hard and do the right things for the right reasons.

Spaghetti alla Bolognese

I chose this recipe because David's favorite meal is spaghetti with meat sauce. Bolognese sauce is a meat-based sauce for pasta originating in Bologna, Italy. This is a variation of a traditional Bolognese sauce that uses hot cherry peppers to spice it up. A traditional Bolognese recipe does not use tomatoes, but I add tomato paste near the end to thicken the sauce and accentuate the rich flavors of this dish. Be careful when adding salt to this dish, since both the pancetta and meat stock have a lot of salt in them. Also, you may not need as much olive oil depending on the fat content of the pancetta.

Ingredients:
½ lb of Beef shoulder, chopped
Pork ¼ lb
Pancetta ¼ lb
3 cloves garlic, sliced
1 yellow onion, diced
1 celery stalk, diced
1 carrot, diced
3 cloves garlic, minced
4 hot cherry peppers, sliced
1 fresh rosemary sprig

1 fresh thyme sprig
2 flat leaf parsley sprigs
½ cup red wine
1 ½ cups chicken stock
3 tablespoons tomato paste (1 small can)
2 tablespoons flour
2 tablespoons olive oil
Cheesecloth
Pasta cooked al dente

Directions:

In pre-heated pan on high heat, thoroughly brown meat, and then scrape into a bowl.

In the same pan on medium to high heat, add olive oil and cook garlic until golden brown, and then discard it. Then use the garlic infused oil in the same pan to brown pancetta for 5 minutes. Add onion, celery, and carrot, then sauté until onion is golden brown. Deglaze with red wine and cook until wine is reduced (about 3 minutes).

Stir in 2 tablespoons flour and cook for 2 minutes before next step.

Add meat, peppers, and stock; bring to boil, let simmer, and season with salt and pepper to taste.

Create a "bouquet garni" with the cheesecloth by rolling together 1 fresh rosemary sprig, 1 fresh thyme sprig, and 2 flat leaf parsley sprigs. Tie the ends with string or strips of the cheesecloth. Place bouquet garni in the sauce.

Simmer and keep covered for up to 3 hours.

Stir in tomato paste and cook for an additional 45 minutes.

Mix with pasta and serve with shaved Parmesan garnish.

RECIPE #9:

THE IMPORTANCE OF A GOOD SOUS CHEF

The Essential Ingredient:
Surround yourself with good people

You can tell a lot about a person by the people they associate with. The most successful people I know surround themselves with people that make them better. Early in his career, Michael Jordan was one of the top scorers in the NBA, yet he played for a losing team. His first NBA Championship did not come until he learned to work with his team. Like basketball, life is a team sport and true success will not come if you are the only talented person on the team. Success, whether it be professional, personal or spiritual, is more likely to be achieved when you have a team that supports you.

Every great chef I have ever met surrounded themselves with great sous chefs. Sous chefs are the direct assistants and proverbial "right hands" to the head chef. They work side by side with the chef and make sure that his or her recipes are properly executed. The really good sous chefs don't just follow orders. They are the "eyes and ears" of the chef and give them invaluable feedback on what is really going on in the kitchen.

The very best chefs I have met know how to develop and mentor great sous chefs. That is why I have so much respect for chefs like Emeril Lagasse and Wolfgang Puck, who not only have great culinary talent, but also have developed so many talented sous chefs that have gone on to be great chefs on their own. On the other hand, I have seen too many great restaurant concepts fail when they open multiple locations only because they could replicate everything but the quality of the food. You can only achieve so much if you are a team of one.

Sous chefs are just as important in your life as they are in the kitchen. Try to think of yourself as the executive chef in charge of your life and your sous chefs are the people you surround yourself with. They are people that you count on to help you create and manage your recipe for life. They are your team of family, friends and co-workers that you rely on every day. Your success largely depends on your ability to surround yourself with a team that makes your recipe a success.

Most people consider team building as something you do at work or in school. But team building is equally, if not more, important with your friends and family. You need great sous chefs in every part of your life.

So how do you find great sous chefs? You have to carefully select them based on your recipe for success. You have to build a team that supports your goals, values, and God-given talents. You need to make sure that your sous chefs have your best interests at heart and support the life you want to live. If you agree that you can tell a lot about a person by the people they associate with, then ask yourself these questions – who are the people on your team and what does that say about you? Do you have the sous chefs that you need to achieve your goals in life? Are the people around you bringing you down or challenging you to be a better person? If you cannot affirmatively answer these questions it may be time for you to start building a team that supports your recipe for life.

I have found that there are six basic elements to building a great team:

First, surround yourself with the best people. As simple as this may sound it is much harder than you would expect. If you really want to surround yourself with the best people, you have to be willing to let people in your life who are better than you are at what they do. Unfortunately, this is counterintuitive to most people's instincts. I have met too many people who prefer to be the smartest person in the room, surrounding themselves with clones that agree with almost everything they say. This usually becomes a recipe for failure because eventually these weak links fail to challenge you to be a better person and ultimately unravel your potential.

Second, align yourself with people that share your values. Do not be overly enamored by intelligence alone. In fact, I believe intelligence by itself is overrated. You can teach a bright person almost anything, but it is nearly impossible to change someone's values. You will find that there are plenty of smart people in this world who lack the wisdom to be truly effective. When deciding who you will surround yourself with, it is necessary to consider intelligence, but you really need to pay attention to the more important attributes — integrity, character and passion. If you value people who do the right things for the right reasons, you need to find people who share your values.

Third, be the example of the principles you want others to emulate. You can demand no more from others than what you are willing to give of yourself. This is so basic it almost goes without saying. You can't be a smoker and tell your children not to smoke, you can't expect people to treat you with respect if you don't first show them respect, and if you want someone to work hard for you then show them what hard work looks like in your deeds and actions. Your ultimate success will depend on how well others embrace your goals and objectives, and nothing motivates people more than someone who leads by example.

Fourth, do not be afraid to challenge your team to prove how good they really are. Most people will rise or fall to whatever expectation you set for them. Do not limit this to the people you work with. You should also apply this to your friends and family, and especially your children. There is a lot to be learned from raising children. In fact, some of the best leaders I have ever worked with were also great parents. They had high expectations for their people and only used discipline as an opportunity to teach. Karen and I raised two children who have both grown into amazing adults. They earned good educations and built solid careers, but most importantly, they are really good and decent people. That was not by accident. Karen taught me everything I know about raising children, and it starts by raising the bar of expectations. From the moment they could talk, Karen spoke to our children like real people with real feelings. "Because I told you so" was not in her vocabulary. She also expected them to be good people and do the right thing. But most of all she emulated the values and character of the person she wanted them to become. In doing so she inspired me to be a better father and a better person.

Fifth, learn to be a great teacher. The most successful team builders I know are teachers. Not necessarily as their profession, but in how they interact with the people they surround themselves with. They are not only good at teaching others, but also understand the importance of learning how to think as a team versus thinking for themselves. "Thinking as a team" means having respect for other people's ideas, the courage to share your thoughts, and creating an environment that encourages a healthy debate. This is contrary to the old-school theory that you should surround yourself with people that can "think for themselves." While it's important to be able to formulate your own thoughts and ideas, it is equally important to have an open mind to the ideas of others.

Sixth and most important of all, you have to truly care about the people you surround yourself with. If you want someone to care about your success, they have to know that you care about them. Caring about someone is more than just a feeling – it's an expression of how you treat others. In fact, caring is the easy part. Showing you care is when the really hard work begins. You have to make time for others, listen to what they have to say, and use every opportunity to teach, grow and learn for yourself. This means caring enough to have an open door, an open mind, and an open heart.

These six attributes for building a great team should apply to everyone you surround yourself with – your friends, family and co-workers. Throughout my life I have been fortunate to be part of some amazing teams that have accomplished a great many things. We defended our country, launched rockets into space, and built skyscrapers that will stand tall for generations. But accomplishments are like plaques on a wall. They only really mean something to the person whose name is on them. I have discovered that true success is found in the happiness that comes from being a part of a team that supports your goals, shares your values, and truly appreciates your God-given talents. By that measure the best team I have ever been a part of is my family.

You are the "chef" in charge of the recipe for your life and a successful life truly depends on having great sous chefs who understand how to help you create a successful recipe. While the other chapters of this book are designed to make you think about what ingredients you need to create your version of success, this chapter is about learning to surround yourself with the people that will get you there. As I said at the beginning of this chapter you can tell a lot about a person by the people they associate with. If you want to be a great chef, make sure you carefully select and develop the right sous chefs!

Veal Osso Buco in Tomato Sauce

*This is one of my favorite dishes and it is perfect for entertaining. This recipe takes quite a bit of effort, so it is best to **have a good Sous Chef** helping you prepare. Once you put it all together you can place it on the stove and slow cook it for hours with little attention required. Dinner parties are a lot more fun when you are not cooking feverishly up to the last minute before your guests arrive.*

The traditional Osso Buco is done Milenaise style that essentially creates a brown sauce that resembles gravy and is served over risotto. I prefer a tomato base sauce that is served over pasta. The secret to this recipe is creating a bed of caramelized red onions that separates the meat from the pan. This will let you slow cook the veal shanks without scorching them. The onions will further caramelize and season the dish. You will need a heavy pot with a lid, preferably a Dutch oven.

Ingredients:

6 veal shanks, 2-3 inches thick
1 red onion, sliced thin
1 carrot, diced
2 stalks celery, diced
3 cloves fresh garlic, minced
1 ½ cups red wine
10 cups chicken stock
4 tomatoes, diced
3 oz tomato paste
1 cup sifted flour
1 teaspoon crushed red pepper
Paprika, garlic powder, salt & pepper
4 tablespoons olive oil
1 lb penne pasta

Directions:

Rub veal with salt, pepper, garlic powder, and paprika; let stand for one hour at room temperature.

Just prior to cooking, coat veal with sifted flour.

Pre-heat large pan on medium to high heat; then add 2 tablespoons olive oil. Brown onion slices on both sides and then line the bottom of a large pot with lid (Dutch oven) with the grilled onions.

In the same pan, set heat to high and brown veal on all sides (about 2-3 min per side). Then remove and set in a Dutch oven with exposed bones facing up.

Set heat to medium to high and brown garlic; then add celery and carrots. When softened, add red wine to deglaze the pan. Let wine cook down until reduced. Add crushed red pepper, salt and pepper. Scrape vegetable mixture into large pot, evenly distributing it around the shanks.

Add broth to pot until almost covering the shanks.

Let cook covered under low-medium heat for at least one hour.

Remove cover, add tomato paste, and diced tomatoes. Cook down for approximately 30 minutes.

Serve over penne pasta.

RECIPE #10:

WHEN LIFE GIVES YOU LEMONS

The Essential Ingredient:
Don't delay spending time with your loved ones

We have all heard the saying, "when life gives you lemons, you need to make lemonade;" however, there will be times in your life when the number of lemons far exceeds your ability to make anything positive out of the experience. These are the times when you find out who your real friends are and, just as important, this is when you will be recognized for how you have impacted the lives of others. In these darkest of hours, you will either be rewarded by those who recognize you as one of their "angels" or ignored by those who do not. What goes around certainly does come back around to either help or haunt you.

While I am very thankful for the many blessings in my life, I have also had a fair share of challenges and tragedies in my life. My mother used to tell me that God only gives you what you can handle; however, there have been many times in my life when I was certain both God and my mother had overestimated me. She knew that no matter how bad things got, all you really need is family, faith, and friends. Even on her deathbed, my mother made a point of reminding me of this.

I was at work one day in Florida when I got the call from my sister that our mother had a massive heart attack. By the time I got to the hospital in Cleveland, she had already been pronounced brain dead, and the doctors were about to take her off life support.
I was so angry with myself for not coming to visit her more often. The year before, she had contracted leukemia, but appeared to be in remission. She had visited us a month earlier, and we all agreed that

we would get together again soon.

Soon: A word we use too often to placate ourselves that we will find the time to make time for those we love. "Let's get together soon." Your child asks, "When can we go to the park again?" and we reply "soon," knowing that "soon" is a metaphor for "when we get around to it." But here I was, standing at my mother's death bed, her frail body pierced by a bunch of tubes and a ventilator just to keep her body in a state of hold, until I could travel across the country to say my final goodbye. Soon had become now, and now was too late.

Shortly after I arrived, my mother's blood pressure quickly dropped to the point it could not register on her monitor. The alarm on her monitor sounded and the nurses and doctor came in to tell us that it was over.

My uncle Richard was a Presbyterian minister in Michigan and he traveled down to be at his sisters' side to say the final prayers. He asked them to leave the room for a minute so we could be alone with her. My uncle gathered us in a circle around her bed and we joined hands, as he led us in prayer. After my uncle finished the prayer, we just stood there weeping and waiting for the doctors to disconnect my mother from the breathing machine.

All of a sudden, my sister started to sing my mother's favorite hymn, *Amazing Grace*. We all joined in.

Then a miracle happened. It was the most miraculous thing I have ever seen, and will always reaffirm my faith that there is a higher power that looks over all of us.

My mother woke up, looked at me, and smiled. Within moments, her heart started beating normally and her blood pressure returned. For the next 40 minutes we talked, we laughed, and we cried. I even joked that she did this just to get me to come home and visit her. When the doctors came in the room, I was so excited and asked them if this meant she was going to make it. You can only imagine my disappointment when the doctor looked at me and said she had read about something like this, but had never witnessed it before. She went on to say there was no reason for my mother to be alive. She had too much damage to her heart and had enough medication in her to put any normal person in a coma. She then said the words that no one ever wants to hear — "Your mother is not going to live."

Unfortunately, the doctor was right and my mother passed away shortly after. I thank God to this day for giving me those few precious moments with her before she died. If there was ever a testimony as to why you should do the really important things now, rather than later, this was certainly it. This is a lesson I hope you never have to learn. Please take my word for it and satisfy those commitments to those you care about sooner, rather than later.

There have been too many calls like these over the years. There have been too many trips to the emergency room, visits to the hospital, and attendance at funerals. We lost my wife's father, both of our grandparents, and too many friends and loved ones. Nobody is immune from the pain and suffering of life on this earth.

You already know about the call I got from Karen when she had the accident that really changed my perspective on life, but you may be surprised to know that the worst call I ever had was actually several years before when she and our daughter had been in another serious automobile accident. Karen's parents were taking her and our daughter away for the weekend, while I was on weekend duty with the Air Force Reserves. Karen and Cara were riding in the back seat of her parents' SUV, when a drunk driver struck them from behind at a speed of more than 100 mph. Although Karen took the brunt of the force from the accident, our daughter was knocked unconscious. When the ambulances arrived, Karen made sure they took care of our daughter and her parents, never mentioning the fact that she was in immense pain. Two days later, we found out that Karen's neck had been broken in two places.

Over the next year, Karen had two major surgeries to fuse disks in her neck and stabilize her spinal cord. She was extremely fortunate the spinal cord had not been severely damaged, and through months and months of intense rehabilitation, she managed to bring her life back to some semblance of normalcy.

However, there were tremendous sacrifices along the way. She had to give up many of the activities she loved, such as water skiing, snow skiing, and anything that could jar or impact her body. But probably the worst impact was that she had to sell the family business. She had built it up to a business that was making millions of dollars per year in sales and was poised for tremendous growth. Karen had it all — she was a loving mother, wonderful wife, and a very successful businesswoman. In the blink of an eye, it was all taken away from her by something completely beyond her control.

As it turned out, the drunken driver who hit their car was fleeing from the police because of an accident he had caused earlier. By the time the highway patrol showed up, the driver fled the scene, eventually catching up to their vehicle, and hit them from behind. After he hit their vehicle, both cars were so mangled that he attempted to flee by foot. Fortunately, some passerby grabbed him and held him until the police arrived. We later learned this drunk driver had a suspended license, no insurance, and two prior convictions for drunk driving. To make matters worse, the judge released him on bail and he never showed up for trial.

Yet the accident had at least one blessing in disguise. As a result of the accident, Karen's mother was given an MRI. Although it did not detect any injuries from the accident, it did reveal the early stages of breast cancer. The doctors were able to take care of it, and her mother has been cancer free for more than 15 years now. Had they not found it this early, she probably would not be alive today. When people tell Karen how sad it is that she had to give up so much, she promptly replies that it was all worth it because it resulted in saving her mother's life.

In addition, when our children were finally old enough to get their drivers' licenses, they became staunch advocates against drinking and driving, and they would make sure none of their friends drove after drinking. Traffic accidents are the leading cause of death among teenagers, and alcohol is too often to blame.

Several years later, Karen managed to build her strength and health back to the point where she wanted to work again. It was not long before she was back full swing. She rebuilt her career and eventually became a very successful marketing executive. Just when it seemed like her life was getting back to normal, tragedy struck again. Karen had that horrific accident just down the street from my office that I described at the very beginning of this book. When we got her to the hospital, we discovered that the force of the accident had severed a previous neck fusion, and destroyed the disks above and below.

Over the next three years, Karen went through three more operations. The doctors had already fused three of her disks, but she still was in intense pain. One thing you have to know about Karen is that she has the most tremendous tolerance for pain of anyone I have ever met, so when she complains about pain, it is severe.

The only remaining option would best be described as a literal "Hail Mary pass" that involved fusing her entire neck into one solid piece. They would have to open her neck up from the front and the back, attach a steel plate with eight screws up the front of her spine, and two steel rods with 16 screws up both sides of the back of her spine. If this did not work, there was nothing else they could do to ease her pain. It was all or nothing.

I researched the Internet and called everyone I knew, searching for the best of the best neurological and orthopedic surgeons. We finally were referred to a doctor who worked with The Buoniconti Fund to Cure Paralysis at the University of Miami. He told her that her spine was so damaged; he would not recommend the surgery.

For the first time in my life, I saw Karen start to lose hope. This was a person who had fought back from a broken neck, endured countless hours of painful and demanding physical therapy, yet never once complained. And now she was giving up. The pain was overwhelming and there was nothing the doctors could do that would give her any relief.

I lost count of the times Karen would look at me in despair and ask, "Do you think I will ever get better?" I would always try to encourage her, but in my heart I knew we were losing the battle. However, I also knew if I gave up hope, she would not survive this ordeal.

There is a dark little secret only someone who has cared for a sick or dying loved one will understand. It is not easy being the "strong one." I cannot begin to express the emotional trauma of watching someone you love experience that kind of pain. It is like watching them slowly drowning, and there is nothing you can do about it. I even felt ashamed for having these feelings because I was not the one experiencing the real pain, yet I knew I was the one being left behind, and the thought of a life without Karen was unbearable.

So against my better instincts, she decided to let our local doctor go ahead with the surgery. It was all or nothing.

The surgery lasted more than six hours. I sat in the waiting room with our children and my wife's mother, praying to God that she would at least survive the operation. When the doctor finally came out, he was surprisingly upbeat. He was confident the surgery was a success and she would get better.

Because of the post-operative pain and healing process, it took several weeks before we saw evidence that the surgery was a success. There was a period of time right after the surgery when we thought it did not work, but eventually her recovery came to light and she started to get better.

Karen was blessed with an indomitable will, and through a lot of hard work and intense physical therapy, Karen finally put her life back together. Two months later, she started back to work part time, and a year later she was able to resume relatively normal activities.

I wanted to share Karen's story with you because here is a person who had experienced serious trauma, not once, but twice in her life, and she had every reason to complain, become resentful, and simply give up. While in her darkest hour, she almost did give up, yet managed to summon the courage to pick herself back up and move forward with her life. Fortunately, she was not alone in her journey. There is an old saying that you reap what you sow, and over her lifetime, Karen has been an "angel" to countless individuals, always giving more than she takes. She certainly changed my life. When she faced this final challenge, there was a line of people waiting to pitch in. I do not know how we would have made it without them, especially our children.

Our daughter, Cara, had recently graduated college. Her dream was to work in the fashion industry, so we sent her to New York where she enrolled in the prestigious Fashion Institute of Technology (FIT). Job opportunities in this industry are extremely hard to come by and the competition is extremely fierce. Just three weeks prior to her mother's operation, Cara finally landed an internship at the New York headquarters for Versace. When we told her about the upcoming surgery, Cara put her dreams on hold, gave up her job, cancelled her classes, and came home to take care of her mother. Cara did not leave her mother's bedside the entire week that Karen spent in the hospital after the surgery. Even the nurses said they had never seen anyone take better care of a loved one. For the next five weeks, she took care of her mother at home. They say the apple does not fall far from the tree, and Cara is no exception.

From the day we met, Karen and I were best friends and soul mates. We did everything together. We were both athletic and we were always on the go. We spent most of our early dates on a racquetball court. At the time, I was playing tournament level racquetball, but I could only beat her two out of three times. She was a real competitor. Now she could no longer do the things we had grown so accustomed to doing together.

We both loved to water ski, and she was one of the few people I trusted to drive the boat when I skied. Not only could she no longer water ski; she could not even drive the boat due to the pounding of the waves. Change was forced upon us. We had to find a way to reinvent our marriage, if it was going to survive.

I have heard a lot of people say you have to work at your marriage. I am certainly no marriage counselor, but I just don't agree with this idea. I firmly believe that relationships are supposed to be fun, not work. If you find yourself having to continually work at something, it is probably not going to last very long. I have known a lot of people over the years who have had good marriages and far too many who have had bad ones. I have met people who got married after a long engagement and others, like us, who fell in love and got married in short order. Living together, abstinence before marriage, similar hobbies and interests, the list of attributes go on and on, yet I have found only one definitive rule for a successful marriage — you must share the same values.

The values that helped Karen and me grow together include faith in God, putting family before all others, and a willingness to compromise for each other. When we were faced with this new challenge, we both had to believe in each other and compromise our lifestyle. I still water ski and snow ski, although it is not nearly as much fun without Karen. Because of this, we have learned to do other things together like cooking.

Karen was always the better cook, but now I had to step into that role. While taking care of her through five operations and the lengthy rehabilitations that followed, I became a pretty good cook too. As soon as Karen was well enough, we started cooking together. Since the day we got married, we always set aside Saturday night as our "date night," when the two of us would go out to dinner. Date night was quickly replaced with cooking night, when the two of us would get in the kitchen with a good bottle of wine, experiment, and create new dishes together. We had reinvented our life around cooking.

A day does not go by that I do not wish for Karen to live a pain-free life and be able to do all of the things she did before her accidents. But when life gives you lemons, you have to find a way to make lemonade, and in our case, we learned to make a lot of great dishes together. We also learned that life is far too short to not take every opportunity to enjoy time with the ones you love. I guarantee you will not be lying in your deathbed wishing you had spent more time at the office. Save yourself from the regret of not spending more time with those who love you. I suggest you do it sooner, rather than later.

Veal Lemon

*There are two reasons why I chose this recipe for this chapter –
because it uses lemons (of course), and most importantly, it's
Karen's favorite recipe. When I make this dish, Karen also makes
her pasta carbonara (see recipe in the back). The two dishes
perfectly compliment each other and take about the same amount of
time to prepare, which makes this the perfect date-night meal – veal
lemon, Karen's carbonara, and a great bottle of wine. Life does not
get much better than this!*

Ingredients:

6 pieces Veal Scaloppini, pounded thin
½ cup sifting flour
1 teaspoon lemon zest
Juice of one lemon
1 tablespoon Italian parsley, chopped
2 tablespoons capers
3 cloves garlic, thinly sliced
¼ cup dry white wine
½cup chicken broth
Paprika, salt and pepper
¼ cup olive oil

Directions:

*Rub the veal with paprika, salt and pepper. Set aside for at least one
hour at room temp. Also remember to zest the lemon and set aside.*

Just prior to cooking, lightly dust veal with sifted flour on all sides.

*Pre-heat a large pan at high heat. Add olive oil and let warm for 2-3
minutes; then add sliced garlic and sear until light golden brown
(about 3 minutes). Stir in the lemon zest and cook for 2-3 minutes.
Strain the oil into a bowl and reserve the cooked garlic and lemon
zest for later.*

Put 2 tablespoons of the lemon and garlic infused oil in the pan. Add veal and brown for 2 minutes on each side. Remove the veal and set aside. If necessary, you can prepare the veal in batches and add more oil with each batch.

With the pan still hot, add the white wine, capers, lemon juice, chicken broth, and the reserved cooked garlic and lemon zest. Scrape the bottom of the pan and allow sauce to come to a boil.

Reduce heat to low and place the meat in the sauce. The sauce should just barely cover the meat. If necessary, add more chicken broth.

Cook until sauce thickens (no more than 5-7 minutes) and serve with parsley garnish.

RECIPE #11:

PASSING THE PLATE

The Essential Ingredient:
Use every opportunity to give back to others

Whether at the dinner table or in a church pew – "passing the plate" is the essence of sharing, and the beauty of sharing is that you always seem to get more back than you gave. Some call it karma, while others call it divine intervention. Some even call it the universal order, but there is a certain amount of truth to the old saying, "What goes around, comes around." I believe that we live in a relatively small world, wherein our paths are so intertwined that our footprints rarely go unnoticed. The evidence of your existence, your actions, and even the words you speak, linger on long after you have left the room. That is why it is so important to think before you speak, especially if your thoughts turn to anger. A friend of mine summed it up best when he told me,

> *"Guard your thoughts because your thoughts will become your words.*
>
> *Watch your words because your words will become your actions.*
>
> *Be careful with your actions because your actions will become your habits.*
>
> *Be mindful of your habits because your habits will define your character.*
>
> *Value your character because your character determines your destiny."*

It is important to understand that your life will be influenced by the good will (or not) of others. The Bible says, "Do unto others as you would have them do unto you." This also implies that others will do for you, as they believe you have done for them. Quite simply, what you do for others will play a huge role in your success in life.

This was a lesson that Franny, my church youth group leader, taught me at an early age. She would gather up our youth group every Saturday morning and haul us down to various churches and community centers in the inner city of Cleveland. We would volunteer as tutors for younger children, visit elderly people in nursing homes, or serve food at homeless shelters. Franny also formed us into a teen choir that traveled the community and eventually across the entire country, singing and performing community service at churches and community centers. She made our lives worthwhile, and in doing so, helped many needy people in the community.

Franny made a point of using every opportunity to open our lives to new experiences. We spent one summer building a school that was wiped out by floods near Hazard, Kentucky. The next summer, Franny took our youth group to La Paz, California. Here we worked for Caesar Chavez, founder of the United Farm Workers union. We built clinics, protested at fields that had unhealthy working conditions, and distributed food and clothing to migrant farm workers. During that summer, I had the privilege of working in Caesar's office, side-by-side with him and his sons.

Caesar Chavez and his family worked tirelessly against overwhelming odds by taking on major growers who did not provide decent working conditions for laborers in the fields. He would gather us to protest at the edge of a field where he knew migrant workers were being mistreated, only to be chased away by thugs with baseball bats. One day we were protesting in front of a supermarket, when one of the patron's shopping carts slid off the curb and fell over. I went to pick it up for her, only to be grabbed by a police officer, slammed down on the pavement, and placed in handcuffs. He thought I knocked her cart over, and only when she corrected him, did he finally let me go. Although it was a minor incident by comparison to what others had gone through, it left a deep impression on me as to the sacrifices Caesar Chavez and his family had to endure.

Many years later, I read about the untimely death of Caesar Chavez, following a long hunger protest. Caesar had given his life in service to those he loved and created a better life for thousands of migrant farm workers.

Throughout my life, I have had numerous opportunities to serve others, and I can tell you, without hesitation, those experiences have given me the most fulfillment in life. Surprisingly enough, some of the most active and meaningful charitable work I have participated in was during my 20 years of military service. You would think that serving our country is more than enough, but military members spend an amazing amount of time and money on local charities. One may be surprised to know that the majority of military service men and women donate a portion of their pay to charities through the Combined Federal Campaign. Every place where I was stationed, the local command had their list of special charitable organizations they supported, including the Special Olympics, Habitat for Humanity, local churches, food banks, and blood drives.

Our country was created on the principle of service to others. Alexis De Tocqueville was a famous 19th-century French nobleman and author who traveled across our country trying to understand this newly minted version of democracy. He particularly admired America's unique spirit of service to others, especially those in need. De Tocqueville remarked that, "When an American asks for the cooperation of their fellow citizens, it is seldom refused; and I have often seen it afforded spontaneously, and with great will."

You see, helping others is not only the right thing to do; it is part of our national heritage.

However, giving back to others should start at home with those you love. I have seen too many "successful" people sacrifice the people who care about them the most. I know this because I was one of them. There have been many times in my life when I allowed work to steal valuable time from my family. Sometimes it is absolutely necessary to create value for you and your family, but even then, it is important to know and respect the impact you have on the lives of those who care about you. Fortunately, Karen is very quick to bring me back down to earth. We all need to pay attention to those we truly care about. The first sign you have lost sight of your priorities is when giving attention to someone you love becomes an inconvenience.

One of the most rewarding experiences I have ever had was helping to create a charitable foundation for our company. Every year, our employees would raise several hundred thousand dollars for the United Way to give to local charities, and our executives would personally contribute much of those dollars. But as we continued to grow, so did the needs of some of our lower-paid employees. Our executive team wanted to create a "safety net" for these employees, which would support them in their time of need and support family-oriented charities in the local communities where our employees live. We met with the leaders of numerous charitable foundations and trusts who were more than happy to share their lessons learned and strategies for building a new foundation. At the end of this process, we created a unique public foundation that raises millions of dollars each year. One of the primary missions of this foundation is to support a private foundation that gives our employees some security when tragedy unexpectedly strikes. Over the years, we have paid for funerals, flown our team members' home to visit a sick or dying relative, and helped countless families keep their homes.

When dealing with family tragedies, it is important to have a process that is swift, thorough, and discreet. When someone is truly in need, they cannot wait for a committee to decide their fate. That is why I personally review and sign all requests, no matter where I am in the world, on business or vacation. The sense of responsibility that comes with making decisions about other people's lives can be very sobering, especially when you have to determine if this was really a tragedy beyond their control and not financial or personal irresponsibility. This experience became an epiphany for me. It has proven, even in our everyday lives, just how much influence we have on the lives of others. Even if you do not hold the pen that signs the approval letter that someone needs, almost every day of your life will present an opportunity to impact someone else's life.

The very first grant we gave was to a housekeeper at one of our resorts. Her son, Joey, was 8 years old and hearing impaired. He had been provided hearing aids by social services, but like most young boys, he managed to lose them, and the government agency would not replace them. Without the ability to hear, Joey started to fail in school, and pretty soon he started acting up in class and exhibiting behavior problems at school and at home. He was on the verge of heading down a very bad path.

We had just announced the start of the foundation and his mother submitted a request for $1,800, to buy new hearing aids. We reviewed the request, spoke to her supervisor, and validated the need. We issued the check.

Several months later, I was holding a staff meeting in my office when the director of the foundation stuck his head in and asked if I could step out for a moment. As I entered the reception area, I noticed a woman standing with a young boy no older than 8 or 9 years old. As soon as I walked into the room, they both lit up and came over to me. The mother introduced herself and told me that her son, Joey, was the recipient of our first foundation grant. Although I approved the grant, I had never met them. She then asked Joey to click his fingers. Joey made a loud clicking sound with his fingers and his face filled up with a big smile. You see, Joey never could click his fingers before because he could not hear the sound that it made. He then gave me a big hug and thanked us for helping him get his hearing back.

Within a few months, Joey was performing better in school. Within a year, he was on the Dean's List for academic achievement. Years later, he won an academic scholarship to a school that specializes in educating children with hearing and sight impairment. Joey's life was changed by a simple stroke of a pen and, in doing so, our lives were forever changed as well. Imagine how something as seemingly insignificant as clicking your fingers became a major milestone in someone else's life.

Just think of all of the things we take for granted in our lives, and, more importantly, think of all of the people we take for granted in our lives. Not just those close to us, but the people we interact with every day — the guy who opens the door for us at work, the lady who cleans our hallways, or the taxi cab driver that picks us up in the rain. We all have the power to spread goodwill to the lives of others, and even in the smallest of increments, improve the world we live in.

One of my all-time favorite movies is "Pay it Forward;" the story of a little boy who comes up with an idea to change the world. His idea is for everyone in the world to find three people who need help and give them something they could not achieve on their own. By the end of the movie, his idea becomes a national movement that spreads kindness across our country like a wildfire.

Just imagine how much better our world would be if "paying it forward" became a reality. This dream will always be challenged by our natural skepticism of strangers in need. How often do we see a vagrant on the side of the road with a "will work for food" sign and think they are probably just looking for drug or alcohol money. Unfortunately many of them are, so we conveniently tell ourselves this as we pass by them, trying not to notice them.

Years ago, while our children were still in elementary school, we were in the drive-thru lane at a fast food restaurant when we spotted a homeless person at the corner with a sign that said, "Need money for food." Our children asked us if we could buy him lunch, so we did. As we pulled out to the street, my wife handed him a sack lunch out the window. He took one look at it, threw it on the ground, and said all he wanted was money. We quickly drove off.

We were concerned that a potentially great lesson for our children, about showing compassion, would now have the opposite effect; so we told them, "Do not let this discourage you from giving to others. For every person like him, there are many more who really need your help."

The truth is, many of these people suffer from mental illness and lack the capacity to properly take care of themselves; plus too many of them are victims of an economic situation beyond their control. Over the years, we have seen more and more people standing on the side of the road asking for help. This is why I find it very difficult to walk past someone who is clearly in need, asking for money. My friends keep reminding me that I am just reinforcing their poor life choices, but in my heart I am hopeful that this person really needs food, even if they are not willing to work for it.

I was recently reminded of this story when my wife received a call about our son, Brian. The night before, Brian and his wife, Nicky, were on their way to a sporting event downtown when he spotted a homeless person panhandling for money. Brian only had $11 in his wallet, which left him one dollar after he paid the parking fee. Brian rolled down his window, pulled out his last dollar, handed it to him, and apologized for not having more to give. The homeless person thanked Brian and said his kind smile was worth more than money. He then said, "All I really need is a pair of socks." A cold front was passing through that night and the temperature was already dropping. Brian looked down and saw that this man had no socks on, so Brian took off his socks and gave them to him.

I was so touched that Brian did this, but more so by the fact that he encountered someone who valued his kindness as much as his donation. There are many good people out there asking for a handout, but really hoping for a hand up. Frankly, I would rather be a foolish optimist that gives money to a stranger hoping they do the right thing, than a skeptic who does nothing. We all need to understand that even the smallest act of kindness can help change someone's life, and we all have the power to make the world a better place. I believe it starts with "paying it forward."

There are many recipes for success, but there are none more fulfilling than what you will gain from giving back to others. What goes around certainly does come back around to us. If you want good things to happen in your life, you have to earn these rewards by making an investment in the lives of others.

Bruschetta with Sun dried Tomato Jam

Great food is even better when it is shared with friends and appetizers are uniquely designed to share. The Italians call it Antipasto (plural antipasti), which means "before the meal". The early Romans are credited with inventing this culinary treat as the first course of their typical three-course meal. Traditional antipasto typically includes a large plate of cured meats, olives, roasted garlic, mushrooms, anchovies, artichoke hearts, and various cheeses that are passed around the table with fresh bread. Another traditional form of antipasto is bruschetta, which is created by placing a mixture of ingredients on top of a toasted slice of bread called a crustini.

Bruschetta is an old-world Italian dish that dates from the 15th century. The word "bruschetta" comes from the Roman word "bruscare," which means, "to roast over coals." It generally consists of grilled slices of bread, rubbed with garlic and olive oil, then topped with various vegetables, meats and cheeses. The best part about making a bruschetta is letting your imagination run wild and creating your own versions.

Bruschetta's are my favorite antipasto, and this is my favorite of all bruschetta's. This dish creates a sweet and tangy jam made from sun-dried tomatoes that are slow cooked in red wine vinegar. You can melt any cheese over the top of this dish, but I have found Brie cheese to provide a nice balance to the intense flavor of the jam.

Ingredients:
Sourdough baguette, sliced on angle ½ inch thick, 8 pieces
½ onion, diced
1 garlic clove, diced
8 oz sun dried tomatoes in oil, drained and sliced
¼ cup red wine vinegar
2 tablespoons sugar

1 teaspoon fresh thyme, minced
1 cup chicken stock
8 slices of Brie cheese
Salt and pepper
2 tablespoons olive oil

Directions:
Pre-heat pan and then add olive oil. Add onion and garlic. Cook until softened (approximately 3-5 minutes).

Add sun dried tomatoes, red wine vinegar, sugar, chicken stock, and fresh thyme. Add salt and pepper to taste. Let cook covered for 20 minutes. Then remove lid and cook additional 10 minutes until thick.

Coat slices of baguette with a light brush of olive and toast until brown.

Spread tomato jam on the baguettes, and then cover with slice of Brie. Bake in oven for 5 minutes at 350 degrees until cheese slightly melts.

Note: In place of Brie cheese you can use 4 oz of goat milk cheese mixed with minced fresh thyme.

RECIPE #12:

BALANCING THE INGREDIENTS

The Essential Ingredient:
Invest in yourself

As I said at the beginning of this book, if you want to find true success, you must first find balance in your life. There is no single definition or method for finding balance in your life because, like success, finding balance is a very personal journey based on your goals, your objectives, and your talents. But I can tell you what it means to be out of balance. Being out of balance simply means you have lost perspective on what is really important to you, and the consequences can be devastating.

The greatest challenge to finding balance comes from the fact that our lives are constantly changing, sometimes without notice. The only thing we really control is how we react to the changes that will inevitably come along. Everything that happens and everyone we meet will become the ingredients that create our recipe for life. If you want your recipe to be a success, you have to figure out how to find balance between the things you cannot control and that which is really important in your life.

As I noted before, your life is a simultaneous journey down three separate paths that lead to your professional, personal, and spiritual lives. With any journey, the first thing you need to do is decide where you are going and how you plan to get there. With your life's journey, you also must decide how much of yourself you will dedicate to each of these paths.

If you spend too much time and energy focused on any one of these paths, you will not likely achieve success with the other two. There are plenty of people who have achieved tremendous professional success by sacrificing their personal or spiritual lives, yet there are just as many people who are so focused on their personal life, they neglect to achieve their true measure of professional or spiritual success. Finding balance means learning how to create a proper equilibrium between these paths.

It is also important to realize that it is possible to achieve great things, yet never experience true success. Conversely, it is just as possible to be successful without achieving great things. You may not win any awards for being a great parent, a good friend, or a considerate person, but you do have unlimited potential to bring happiness and fulfillment to yourself and others. If happiness is one of the ingredients in your recipe for success, you must find balance in your life.

Finding balance in your life is not only necessary for your mental health, but just as important, it will improve your physical health. We live in the most hectic and stressful times in the history of mankind. It all started with the personal computer; I know this because I am a techno-junkie.

I bought my first computer soon after they hit the shelves in the early 1980's. Since then, I have "upgraded" myself hundreds of times to almost every electronic gadget and toy you can imagine. I have managed to automate almost everything in my life, from my house to the office, but I have to admit that all of these "upgrades" have downgraded the quality of my personal life.

These advances in technology are making it harder and harder to truly separate us from the stress-drivers in our lives. We spend more and more of our lives living and communicating in a virtual world that operates at light speed. Just imagine where we will be 20 years from now.

I used to be excited about where advances in technology were taking us, but now I am not so sure. This "advancement" has exacted a tremendous toll on our personal lives. Too often, our only interactions with others are via emails, text messaging, and instant messaging. We have created social networks that allow us to connect with millions of people in our own virtual world. Why should you write someone when you can send an email? Why should you call someone when you can text them? What does it say about you when your most prolific source of information comes from a Twitter account? Unfortunately, this is a world filled with knowledge, yet desperately lacking in wisdom. With so much information flowing in and out of our lives, it is almost impossible to take the time to express true human emotions or to genuinely reflect before you respond. We are in a race against time, compounded by an endless flow of information that never ends.

That is why finding balance in your life is now more important than ever. We face dire consequences if we do not learn how to take care of ourselves mentally, spiritually, and physically. Over the years, I have lost a great many friends and loved ones, yet I have not seen one of them leave this world wishing they had sent more emails or spent more time at the office.

The first step to finding balance in your life is to understand what "balance" really means to you. There are countless tools available that you can use to do this. I recently ran a web search on "finding balance in your life" and found more than 46 million responses; but you really do not need a guidebook for this exercise. All you really need to do is sit down with a piece of paper and make a list of what you want to do with your life. Then make a list of what you truly consider to be important, including the people that matter most and the things that really make a difference. Finally, make a list of what brings joy and contentment to you. Place all three lists side by side, take a step back, and examine the results. You now have a very clear picture of what you want to do, what you consider to be important, and what makes you happy.

The next step to finding balance is to set realistic expectations for your life. This means you have to accept that you will not be able to maintain perfect balance at all times. There will be times when you lose your balance, and times when you fall down. There will even be times when you will need to sacrifice your personal life to do what is necessary to succeed at work or school. The key is to recognize when you are out of balance and effectively communicate with the people you truly care about. Make sure they understand that what you are doing is necessary, and make a commitment to give back to them in other ways.

The most important step in finding balance in your life is to take time to invest in your own life. The most successful people I know are the ones who have their own special place they can escape to, a place to clear their minds and recharge their batteries. Some of them call it a hobby, others call it a sport, and still others call it their true avocation in life. You must have something in your life that helps you rejuvenate your soul and rekindle your passion for life.

I was recently reminded of this after reading a newspaper article someone wrote about her experience boarding a commercial flight. After "teaching" everyone how to put on their seatbelts, the flight attendant proceeded to show the passengers how to put on oxygen masks just as we have all seen hundreds of times before. Most flight attendants begin by saying, "In the event of an emergency, put on your oxygen mask before trying to help someone else." On this particular day, the flight attendant said something that put this whole exercise in perspective. She said, "You can't save the ones closest to you if you are already suffocating." In essence, she was saying there would be times in your life when taking care of yourself is not an act of selfishness.

Music has always been the source of balance in my life. Most of my mother's siblings were either musicians or vocalists. When the family got together, they would break out the instruments and sing and play until all hours of the night. When I was 8 years old, my mother gave me an old guitar that had belonged to one of my uncles. I found an old Ernie Ball guitar book, and pretty soon I learned enough cords to make my own music. There were many times while I was growing up when my only escape was to go in my room, turn off the lights, and play my guitar in the dark. I would imagine myself playing a concert in front of a grand audience. Pretty soon the world around me did not seem like such a bad place after all.

Later in life, as I hitchhiked across the country, and during my early days in the military, my guitar was my faithful companion; my music was my escape from life's daily frustrations; music rejuvenated my soul.

When Karen entered my life, I found balance in the things we could do together. At first it was sports, but when the events of her life altered our path, we learned to cook together. The great thing about cooking is that it is nearly impossible to create a great dish, yet think about the negative or stressful things in our lives at the same time.

That is why it is essential to find a way to disconnect from it all and find a place that rejuvenates your soul. Find a hobby, activity or sport that drives your passion, allowing you to regain the emotional energy you need to be successful. When you find yourself being tugged in different directions, try to remember what that flight attendant said. "You can't save the ones closest to you if you are already suffocating!"

Jalapeño Balsamic Wine Reduction

*If anything exemplifies my cooking style, it is combining sweet and spicy elements to a dish to accentuate the true flavors of peppers (not just the heat). Most peppers have a wonderful flavor that can be masked by the fire that hits your tongue when you bite into them. I learned this from a Mexican neighbor of mine when I was very young. My mother used to grow her own jalapeno peppers, and we were in the backyard with our neighbor picking vegetables when he encouraged me to try a raw jalapeno. I bit into one and thought my mouth had caught on fire. I immediately gulped down a glass of water, which only made it worse. He then handed me a pack of sugar and told me to coat my tongue with it. The fire in my mouth subsided almost immediately. That was my first lesson in **balancing the ingredients!***

This is a very simple sauce to make and it is excellent for use on meats, especially a pepper encrusted steak au poivre. Since the sugars in the balsamic vinegar and the jam counteract the heat from the pepper, it is not really that spicy, so I would encourage someone who does not normally like spicy foods to try this sauce.

Ingredients:
¼ stick butter
2 fresh jalapeños, sliced thin
1/8 cup balsamic vinegar
¼ cup port wine
2 tablespoons berry jam

Directions:
In a pre-heated pan on medium to high heat, melt butter.

As soon as the butter foams, add the jalapeños and cook on both sides until lightly browned (about 3-4 minutes).

Stir in balsamic vinegar, port wine, and jam and cook until reduced (about 5-8 minutes).

Reduce to simmer until ready to serve.

THE FINALE:

PLATING THE DISH

Most chefs are familiar with the term "plating the dish," which refers to placing your creation on the plate just prior to serving. It is the culmination of your hard work, creativity, and technical expertise. It is also your last chance to influence the outcome, to put your dish out there for everyone to see, and make that first impression a lasting one.

This is your chance to create your own recipe for success. You can use any or all of the ingredients I have provided, but in the end you have to season your dish to your taste. It is your recipe and you have to "eat" what you create. You must to decide what is important to you and what you are willing to do to achieve it.

Looking back on my life thus far, there have been numerous "recipes for success" along the way. All I had to do was find the right ingredients. Although my parents were always broke, I eventually learned we were never really poor; we just did not have money. Money was something you could earn, and I have proven that. I also learned the importance of a strong education. Although my family could not afford to pay for my education, I managed to get educated in ways most people will never experience. I was also fortunate to live in a country where opportunity is abundant, and all you have to do is add hard work and the right attitude to give yourself the opportunities to succeed.

There is something very interesting about achieving one of your life's goals. While you know you should be happy and truly satisfied that you climbed that mountain, earned that degree, or got that promotion you worked for so tirelessly, sometimes obtaining a goal is not nearly as satisfying as the journey you took to get there. In fact, each time in life I have "climbed that mountain" and achieved my goal, I find myself looking back and realizing the real joy in my life was working towards the goal, not the goal itself. That is why I believe it is important to measure your success by the road you traveled and people you have met, rather than the destination. While it is very important to achieve your goals, do not lose the opportunity to enjoy the ride along the way.

The Greek philosopher, Aristotle, from the 3rd century BC, best summed it up when he said, "Of course there is no formula for success except perhaps an unconditional acceptance of life and what it brings." Even the ancient Greeks knew that life's success was determined by the journey, not the destination.

I have found a great amount of success in my life. The greatest of all are the relationships I have with my wife and children, but I also have much, much more to do with my life. There are still mountains to be climbed, businesses to be created, and experiences to be had. With every bad thing that has happened in my life, I have managed to find things I can learn and grow from, because the day we stop growing is the day we start dying.

Mark Twain said it best, "Twenty years from now you will be more disappointed by the things that you didn't do than by the ones you did do. So throw off the bowlines. Sail away from the safe harbor. Catch the trade winds in your sails. Explore. Dream. Discover."

So I encourage you to take my personal recipe and create your own recipe for success based on your life, your dreams, your talents, and your ambitions. ***Bon Appétit!***

My List of Essential Ingredients:

Accept responsibility for your life

Work hard

Respect the differences of others

Stand up for what is right

Recognize the "angels" in your life

Be loyal

Get paid doing what you enjoy

Be true to your values and value others

Surround yourself with good people

Don't delay spending time with your loved ones

Use every opportunity to give back to others

Invest in yourself

ANTIPASTI
(APPETIZERS)

ASIAN CHICKEN WINGS

BRUSCHETTA WITH MUSHROOMS & CARAMELIZED ONIONS

BRUSCHETTA WITH FIG & HAZELNUT JAM

BRUSCHETTA WITH GOAT CHEESE & PROSCUITTO

BRUSCHETTA WITH SHAVED BEEF AND GORGONZOLA

BRUSCHETTA WITH SUN DRIED TOMATO JAM

BRUSCHETTA WITH TOMATO, BASIL, AND GARLIC

CARAMELIZED ONION AND GOAT CHEESE TOAST

FRIED CALAMARI

GUACAMOLE

PIZZA DOUGH

POT STICKERS

ROASTED CIPOLLINI ONIONS

ROASTED GARLIC

STUFFED MUSSELS

SUMMER ROLLS

THAI LETTUCE WRAPS

ASIAN CHICKEN WINGS

This is a real easy appetizer to make that will impress your guests. It is best to prepare this dish using a wok; however, if you don't have one, you can use a large skillet. Once the sauce starts to thicken, stir constantly to prevent sticking or scorching. You can also finish the cooked wings on a grill.

Ingredients:
2 dozen chicken wings
¼ cup ketchup
¼ cup soy sauce
2 tablespoons chili paste
1 ½ teaspoons salt
2 tablespoons brown sugar
1 inch grated ginger root
4 cloves minced garlic
2 tablespoons sesame seeds
1 ½ teaspoons ground coriander seeds
1 teaspoon ground cumin
3-4 tablespoons olive oil
½ yellow onion, diced
1 cup chicken broth
3 tablespoons cilantro, chopped

Directions:
In a large bowl, mix the ketchup, soy sauce, chili paste, salt, brown sugar, ginger, garlic, sesame seeds, coriander seeds, and cumin.

Preheat oven to 400 degrees.

Rinse and dry the wings and place them in a separate bowl. Add 2 tablespoons olive oil, salt and pepper and toss the chicken wings until they are thoroughly covered.

In a large pre-heated wok or pan on high heat, add remaining oil and brown wings thoroughly on all side (about 10-12 minutes).
When the wings are brown, you may want to drain off some of the excess grease before the next step.

Add the diced onions to the wings and continue turning the wings until the onions are softened (approximately 3-5 minutes).

Add the sauce mixture to wok and continue stirring the chicken until brown on all sides (about 10-15 minutes). Add chicken broth as necessary to prevent wings from sticking or scorching.

Place in oven for 15 minutes.

Remove from oven when wings are crisp. Mix with fresh chopped cilantro and serve.

BRUSCHETTA

Bruschetta is an old-world Italian dish that dates from the 15th century. The word bruschetta is derived from the Roman word bruscare, which means, "to roast over coals." It generally consists of grilled slices of bread, rubbed with garlic and olive oil, then topped with various vegetables, meats and cheeses. Bruschetta is the ultimate finger food and great for entertaining company because you can prepare most of the pieces in advance; then construct the final dish right before your company arrives. The best part about making a bruschetta is letting your imagination run wild and creating your own versions. Here are a few of my favorites:

BRUSCHETTA WITH MUSHROOMS & CARAMELIZED ONIONS

Ingredients:
- Sourdough baguette, sliced on angle ½ inch thick, 8-12 pieces
- ½ lb thin sliced mushrooms (I prefer Shitake, but you can use almost any mushroom)
- ¼ cup Italian parsley, diced
- ¼ cup tomatoes, diced
- ½ yellow onion, chopped
- 4 oz Boursin cheese (Boursin cheese is similar to a soft cream cheese)
- 4 oz sliced Provolone
- ¼ cup dry white wine
- ½ cup chicken broth
- Crushed red pepper
- Salt and pepper
- 1 tablespoon unsalted butter
- 1 tablespoon olive oil

Directions:
To create the crustini, toast slices of baguette, then add slices of Provolone, and place under broiler until crispy. Set aside to cool.

In a pre-heated pan, melt the butter with the olive oil. Add onions and a pinch of crushed red pepper. Cook until onions are softened (approximately 5 minutes).

Add mushrooms and cook 3-5 min until softened. Then deglaze with white wine.

Add broth and cook down until liquid slightly reduces. Then stir in tomatoes and parsley. Cook 3-5 min. Add salt and pepper to taste.

Arrange the crustini in a pie shaped pattern on a plate, then lay mushroom and onion mix in center of plate.

Top the end of each crustino with a teaspoon of Boursin cheese and serve.

ఆ BRUSCHETTA WITH FIG ౨ & HAZELNUT JAM

Ingredients:
- Sourdough baguette, sliced on angle ½ inch thick, 8 pieces
- 1 cup sugar
- ½ cup water
- 2 tablespoons of Brandy
- 12 fresh figs, sliced in half
- 4 oz hazelnuts
- 2 oz shredded Pecorino Romano cheese
- 1 green apple sliced thin
- Olive oil

Directions:
Bring water to boil, and then add sugar and brandy. Turn off heat and soak the figs in sugar water for 10 minutes.

Pour mixture in food processor, add hazelnuts, and process into a thick consistency.

Lightly brush baguette slices with olive oil and toast in oven at 400 degrees until slightly brown. Add shredded Pecorino Romano and let melt, and then remove from oven.

When cheese cools to a hard surface, coat baguette slices with thick layer of jam and one thin slice of apple.

BRUSCHETTA WITH GOAT CHEESE & PROSCUITTO

Ingredients:
- Sourdough baguette, sliced on angle ½ inch thick, 8 pieces
- ½ lb thin Serrano ham
- Calamatto Black olives, pitted and sliced thin
- 1 handful of Italian Parsley, minced
- 4 oz of Humbolt Fog Goat cheese
- 1 tablespoon grape seed oil
- 1 tablespoon olive oil
- Salt and pepper

Directions:
In a bowl, let Goat cheese sit at room temperature, approximately 20 minutes until softened, then mix with minced parsley, salt & pepper.

In broiler, toast ham until crisp.

Coat slices of baguette with a light brush of olive oil and toast until brown.

Cover Baguette slices with cheese mix, drizzle with grape seed oil, and bake for 5 min at 400 degrees.

Remove and add olive slices and ham.

BRUSCHETTA WITH SHAVED BEEF & GORGONZOLA

Ingredients:
- Sourdough baguette, sliced on angle ½ inch thick, 8 pieces
- 4 oz sirloin steak, approximately 1 inch thick
- ¼ cup Gorgonzola cheese, grated
- 1 small tomato, diced
- 1 small bell pepper, diced
- 4 green onions, diced
- 2 oz of sweet balsamic vinegar
- 1 oz Italian salad dressing
- 8 leaves of fennel
- 3 oz of grated Parmesan cheese
- Salt and pepper
- Olive oil

Directions:
Heat oven to 400 degrees. Salt and pepper steak, and then bake until medium rare (approximately 5 minutes). Remove steak and let stand until cool.

Shave steak into thin slices, 2 inches long.

Make pesto by mixing tomato, bell pepper, green onions, balsamic vinegar, Italian dressing, salt and pepper.

Coat slices of baguette with a light brush of olive oil and toast until brown. Then cover with layer of Gorgonzola cheese.

Place slice of steak on cheese, then cover with pesto, and sprinkle with Parmesan cheese.

Add slice of fennel over top and serve.

⊂℞ Bruschetta with ℞⊃ Sun dried Tomato Jam

This is my favorite of all bruschetta's that uses a sweet and tangy jam made from sun-dried tomatoes. You can melt any cheese over the top of this dish, but I have found Brie cheese to provide a nice balance to the intense flavor of the jam.

Ingredients:
- Sourdough baguette, sliced on angle ½ inch thick, 8 pieces
- ½ onion, diced
- 1 garlic clove, diced
- 8 oz sun dried tomatoes in oil, drained and sliced
- ¼ cup red wine vinegar
- 2 tablespoons sugar
- 1 teaspoon fresh thyme, minced
- 1 cup chicken stock
- 8 slices of Brie cheese
- Salt and pepper
- 2 tablespoons olive oil

Directions:
Pre-heat pan, and then add olive oil. Add onion and garlic. Cook until softened (approximately 3-5 minutes).

Add sun dried tomatoes, red wine vinegar, sugar, chicken stock, and fresh thyme. Add salt and pepper to taste. Let cook covered for 20 minutes. Then remove lid and cook additional 10 minutes until thick.

Coat slices of baguette with a light brush of olive oil and toast until brown.

Spread tomato jam on the baguettes, and then cover with slice of

Brie. Bake in oven for 5 minutes at 350 degrees until cheese slightly melts.

Note: In place of Brie cheese you can use 4 oz of goat milk cheese mixed with minced fresh thyme.

BRUSCHETTA WITH TOMATO, BASIL & GARLIC

This is a classic version of bruschetta. I recommend using a colander to strain as much of the juices as possible from the tomatoes. I really like garlic, but you may want to try this with less garlic the first time.

Ingredients:
- Sourdough baguette, sliced on angle ½ inch thick, 8 pieces
- 4 large vine ripe tomatoes, peeled and diced
- 4 garlic cloves, diced
- ¼ cup virgin olive oil
- ½ teaspoon salt
- ½ teaspoon fresh ground black pepper
- 1 pinch of crushed red pepper
- ¼ cup basil leaves, minced
- 2 tablespoons grated Parmesan cheese

Directions:
Blanch tomatoes in boiling water for 30 seconds then immerse in cold water. Core and peel tomatoes.

Dice tomatoes, remove, and discard seeds and juice.

Toss tomatoes with basil, olive oil, and garlic. Add crushed red pepper, salt, and pepper. Let marinate for at least 1 hour in the refrigerator.

Coat slices of baguette with a light brush of olive oil and toast until brown.

Cover baguettes with mixture and garnish with grated Parmesan cheese.

⨯⨯ CARAMELIZED ONION & ⨯⨯ GOAT CHEESE TOAST

This is a very simple appetizer to prepare; yet it is one of the most requested appetizers that I make. The key is to fully caramelize the onions, and use a really good Goat cheese. The honey will counteract and balance the intense flavor of the cheese. Try cutting these in quarters and serve on an appetizer plate.

Ingredients:
- 4 thin slices of sourdough bread
- 4 ounces of Goat cheese
- 1 sweet onion sliced thin
- 1 tablespoon olive oil
- ¼ cup dry white wine
- 2 tablespoons honey
- 2 teaspoons olive oil

Directions:
Make sure that Goat cheese is refrigerated and hard enough to slice.

In pre-heated pan, add olive oil. Add onions and cook until golden brown (fully caramelized). This should take approximately 20 minutes. When onions are brown, add sugar and deglaze with white wine. Cook until all of the liquid is reduced. Remove onions and set aside.

Pre-heat oven to 400 degrees.

Toast bread and then cover with caramelized onions. Cover onions with slices of goat cheese and drizzle with honey.

Bake in oven until cheese slightly turns golden brown. Let cool for 5 minutes before serving.

FRIED CALAMARI

This unique approach to calamari uses finely ground graham cracker crumbs to create the crust. Proper oil temperature is the key to preventing fried dishes from getting greasy. That is why I recommend you get a good oil thermometer.

Ingredients:
- 1 lb fresh calamari, sliced in ½ inch rings
- 4 cups olive oil
- 1 cup flour
- 1 cup graham cracker crumbs, finely ground
- 1 teaspoon kosher salt
- 1 cup buttermilk
- 1 cup Marinara sauce (see recipe)

Directions:
Mix calamari in bowl with buttermilk. Cover and refrigerate overnight.

In large bowl, mix flour and graham crackers.

Heat olive oil to 360 degrees minimum.

Salt rings, dip in flour mix, and place in hot grease. Cook until golden brown. Remove and place on plate, covered with paper towel to absorb excess grease.

Recommend serving with Marinara sauce for dipping

 GUACAMOLE

This is a simple dish that we learned from a small family-style Mexican restaurant that prepared this dish tableside. The key to a great guacamole is getting the right consistency with the mashed avocados. I prefer to leave them a little lumpy. Also, make sure you drain off all of the tomato juices; otherwise this dish will be too runny. Finally, not all jalapeños are created equal. If you do not like spicy food, start with ½ of a jalapeño, mix it in and add more if necessary.

Ingredients:
- 6 avocados softened to ripe
- ¼ cup cilantro, diced
- 1-2 jalapeño peppers, minced
- ½ red onion, diced
- 2 tomatoes, diced; juice and seeds removed
- Juice of 1 lime
- Kosher salt

Directions:
Slice avocados in half, remove pit, and scoop into a large bowl (a large spoon will work well to scoop out the avocados). Using a potato masher, mash avocados into a thick, yet slightly lumpy consistency.

Stir in cilantro, tomatoes, jalapeño peppers, and onion. Squeeze in lime and salt to taste.

ᚙ Pizza Dough ᚙ

There are not many dishes that are as fun to make and inspire creativity like making your own pizza. Believe it or not, the easiest part is making the dough. This is a very basic recipe that produces a good thin-crust pizza when rolled out on a hard surface. The best pizzas are made in wood- or charcoal-fired ovens. You can replicate this technique with a good pizza stone placed on your outdoor gas or charcoal grill. Most of the popular kitchenware stores sell them for under $50. Place the stone on your already heated grill and allow it to pre-heat for about 15-20 minutes.

You should also get a "pizza peel" to transfer the pizza to the stone. Since dough will stick to most surfaces, you should sprinkle corn meal on the pizza peel before applying the dough and pizza ingredients. Also, you can achieve a crispier pizza if you lightly brush the rolled out dough with olive oil before applying any ingredients.

My favorite pizza is a simple Margherita pizza that consists of a thick layer of my marinara sauce, followed by a layer of shredded mozzarella. Then spread slices of vine-ripe tomatoes and fresh basil on top of the cheese. But the great thing about pizza is letting everyone make up his or her own list of ingredients.

Once you have your pizza creation ready, slide it on the pizza stone, cover the grill and 10-15 minutes later you will have a hot, crisp pizza ready to go.

Ingredients:
- 2 cups flour
- ½ cup warm water
- ½ cup Pellegrino water
- 2 teaspoons yeast

- 3 tablespoons olive oil
- 1 tablespoon sugar
- 2 teaspoons kosher salt
- ½ cup corn flour

Directions:

Mix the yeast and sugar in warm water and set aside.

Put 2 cups of all-purpose flour into a food processor with the salt. Mix and add 3 tablespoons of olive oil.

With mixer still running, add yeast mixture, then Pellegrino and let blend until the dough forms.

Remove and knead until smooth over lightly floured counter, about one minute. If dough is too sticky, add flour one tablespoon at a time to achieve desired consistency. If it is too dry, add one tablespoon at a time.

Separate dough into two balls, lightly coat with olive oil and wrap with plastic wrap. Refrigerate for at least 2 hours, preferably overnight.

You can also freeze dough balls for later use (recommend using airtight freezer bag for long term storage).

2 hours before using, remove plastic wrap and place dough in an oiled bowl, cover with plastic wrap and let it rise in a warm, draft free area.

When preparing pizza dough, sprinkle flour on a hard surface and knead dough into a circular shape. A rolling pin may also be used. If you are feeling adventurous you can try tossing your dough by first spreading it over the knuckles of your clenched fist. Then push it into the air with a twist of your wrist, and let land back on your fist.

With each toss the dough should spin and relax into a slightly larger shape, eventually requiring both fists to manipulate the dough.

When you are ready to make your pizza, liberally sprinkle corn flour over your pizza peel or baking sheet before rolling it out. This will prevent the pizza from sticking to the pan.

Finally, once the dough is rolled out on the pizza peel and before adding any ingredients, lightly brush the surface of the dough with olive oil. This will allow the dough to cook evenly and create a crispy, golden-brown crust.

❦ POT STICKERS ❧

Pot stickers are Chinese dumplings that consist of a ground meat and/or vegetable filling, wrapped into a thinly rolled piece of dough, which is then sealed by pressing the edges together or by crimping. They can be steamed, fried, or grilled. Pot Stickers are easy to make and present another great opportunity to flex your creativity. Try different meats and vegetables to create your own version. For the dough, you can usually find good wonton wrappers in the fresh produce section of your local grocery store. Just a touch of water on the edges of the wonton acts like a glue that will hold the edges together.

Ingredients:
- ¼ cup dried shitake mushrooms
- ½ teaspoon salt
- ¼ lb ground pork
- ½ cup minced fresh garlic chives
- 1 tablespoon light soy
- 1 tablespoon sesame oil
- 2 teaspoons rice wine
- 2 teaspoons fresh ginger, finely minced

- 1 clove garlic, minced
- 2 tablespoons cornstarch
- ½ teaspoon ground white pepper
- 45 thin round wonton wrappers
- 2 tablespoons canola oil
- 1 cup low sodium chicken broth
- Ginger-soy dipping sauce (see recipe under sauces)

Directions:

Soak the dried mushrooms in warm water for 30 min. Drain, remove stems, and mince.

In a large bowl, mix mushrooms, pork, chives, soy, sesame oil, rice wine, ginger, garlic, corn starch, and white pepper.

Fill wontons with meat mix, brush edges with water, fold over, and pleat.

Place pot stickers on lightly floured baking sheet.

In large non-stick pan, heat the canola oil. Brown pot stickers 3-4 min, then add chicken broth, cover and let steam 4-5 min.

Transfer to platter, cover and keep warm in oven at 180 degrees until ready to serve.

ROASTED CIPOLLINI ONIONS

Cipollini onions (pronounced chip-oh-LEE-nee) are small, flat onions that are sweeter than garden-variety white or yellow onions. Their size and shape lends them well to roasting, and they are the perfect accompaniment to rack of lamb or a char grilled steak.

Ingredients:
- 1 dozen Cipollini onions, peeled and whole
- ⅓ cup balsamic vinegar
- 2 tablespoons olive oil
- Salt and pepper

Directions:
In small baking dish, mix onions with balsamic vinegar, olive oil, salt and pepper.
Bake uncovered for 1 hour at 400°.

ROASTED GARLIC

Roasted garlic is delicious on toasted French bread or as a side dish for most grilled meats.

Ingredients:
- 6 garlic bulbs
- 1/2 cup olive oil
- Salt and pepper

Directions:
Pre-heat oven to 300 degrees.

Trim top of garlic bulbs without cutting into cloves and remove outer shell of paper to expose the cloves.

Place heads in shallow roasting pan and drizzle with olive oil.

Season with salt and pepper.

Cover with foil and roast for 1 hour.

Uncover and baste cloves with pan juices for 15 minutes longer.

❦ STUFFED MUSSELS ❧

This is another simple appetizer to make that will really impress your guests. The key is to find live, fresh mussels. You should be able to tell a fresh mussel by its smell — it should smell like a clean beach. As with all shellfish, mussels should be checked to ensure they are still alive just before they are cooked. A simple test is that live mussels, when exposed to air, will shut tightly when disturbed. An open mussel that does not respond is dead, and must be discarded. Mussels quickly become toxic after dying. If a shell is already closed, you can gently pry it open and check it.

Just prior to cooking, thoroughly rinse the mussels in water and remove "the beard." Once you remove the beard, the mussel will start to die. Mussel shells will open when cooked, revealing the cooked soft parts.

Ingredients:
- 2 ½ lbs fresh mussels
- 2 lemons quartered
- 4 garlic cloves
- 3 tablespoons white wine
- 4 tablespoons olive oil
- 2 ½ cups white bread crumbs
- Sea salt and fresh ground black pepper
- Lemon wedges

Directions:
Pre-heat oven to 425 degrees.

Discard any mussels that are broken or do not close when sharply tapped.

Rinse mussels in cold water, removing beards.

Put lemon, garlic, white wine, and mussels in pan, cover and cook at high heat for 5 minutes until shells open. Shake pan occasionally. Discard any mussels that do not open.

Remove mussels, reserve broth.

Loosen mussels, but leave in shell, and discard other half of shell. Strain broth into a bowl and then mix in olive oil, breadcrumbs, salt and pepper.

Place mixture on each mussel.

Bake about 7 min until golden brown.

.

SUMMER ROLLS

A summer roll is a Vietnamese food that resembles an un-fried egg roll. Summer rolls are served cold, and are much healthier than their fried cousins. You will start with freshly cooked sheets of rice paper, and roll together a variety of vegetables with pork, chicken or seafood. This is another dish that lends itself to your creativity. I prefer shrimp rolls, but you can try adding fresh mint leaves, or substituting the shrimp with cooked lobster, chicken, or pork. I also add slivers of sweet cherry peppers, but you can substitute any hot or sweet pepper to enhance the flavor of this dish.

Ingredients:
- 6 sheets of rice paper
- ¼ lb of rice noodles
- 6-8 shrimp
- 6 mint leaves
- 6 stalks of cilantro
- 6 pieces of green leaf lettuce

- 4 sweet cherry peppers sliced in slivers
- 3 green onions, diced

Directions:
Peal the raw shrimp then boil them until cooked. Set in refrigerator and let cool. Remove shrimp and split in half. Set aside.

Put rice noodle in boiling water until cooked and set aside.

Note: the following steps should be done very quickly to keep rice paper from setting up and sticking to plate.

Lay a clean dishtowel over a plate. Take one sheet of rice paper and drench it quickly in warm water (approximately 30 seconds). Then delicately place the sheet of rice paper on top of the dishtowel.

Take a piece of green leaf lettuce, 3 mint leaves, a piece of cilantro, 4 shrimp, sweet cherry pepper slices, and place them on the edge of the rice paper.

Take the rice paper with all of the ingredients inside and roll halfway. Fold the ends over and then finish rolling.

❦ Thai Lettuce Wraps ❧

This is a great dish to have when you are sitting around a table with friends and family. I call it the Asian version of fajitas. I like to place the meat mix in a bowl and place a few different dips around the table for everyone to try (see the recipe for Ginger-Soy dipping sauce).

Ingredients:
- One head of Iceberg lettuce
- 6 Chinese black mushrooms
- 2 tablespoons Oyster Sauce
- 1 tablespoon each light & dark soy sauce
- 1 teaspoon Asian sesame oil
- ½ teaspoon sugar
- ½ teaspoon corn starch
- 1/8 teaspoon ground white pepper
- 1 large egg
- 2 tablespoons canola oil
- 1 tablespoon ginger
- 2 cloves garlic
- ½ lb minced chicken
- ¼ lb minced pork
- ½ cup minced canned bamboo shoots
- 6 water chestnuts, minced (canned)
- ¼ cup hoisin sauce
- 3 tablespoons green onions, diced
- Pine nuts

Directions:
Cut out stem of lettuce and immerse head in bowl of very cold water for 30 minutes.

Take 20 leaves and trim into cups, then refrigerate.

Soak mushrooms for 10-15 minutes, drain and then mince.

In a large bowl, mix the oyster sauce, dark & light soy, sesame oil, corn starch, sugar, white pepper, and egg. Set aside.

In a pre-heated wok, heat canola oil to very hot. Add ginger & garlic and fry until golden brown. Add the chicken & pork and brown for 5-7 min. Drain off any excess juice.

Return pan to high heat; add bamboo shoots, water chestnuts, & mushrooms. Stir fry until moisture is removed (3-4 min).

Stir in oyster mix and cook until thickened. Remove from heat.

In a small bowl, mix hoisin sauce with 1 tablespoon warm water.

Place meat mix in lettuce, drizzle with hoisin sauce, and garnish with green onion and pine nuts.

Zuppe e Insalate
(Soups and Salads)

CHOPPED VINAIGRETTE SALAD WITH SHAVED CARROTS & CURRY

CRAWFISH & ANDOUILLE SAUSAGE GUMBO

FRENCH ONION SOUP

ITALIAN TOMATO PASTA SOUP

LOBSTER BISQUE

SPICY BLACK BEAN SOUP

Chopped Vinaigrette Salad with Shaved Carrots & Curry

Ingredients:
- 1 head romaine lettuce, chopped
- 4 carrots shaved
- 2 pears sliced ¼" thick
- ¼ cup Italian parsley, chopped
- ½ cup extra virgin olive oil
- ¼ cup white wine vinegar
- 2 tablespoons honey
- 1 tablespoon curry powder
- 1 teaspoon salt
- 1 teaspoon fresh ground pepper

Directions:
In a large bowl, toss the lettuce, carrots, pears and parsley.

In a food processor, add wine vinegar, honey, curry powder, salt and pepper. While processor is running, slowly pour in olive oil and blend to a smooth consistency.

Pour over salad and toss.

Crawfish & Andouille Sausage Gumbo

Gumbo is a Louisiana soup that brings together the rich cuisines of regional Indian, French, Spanish, and African cultures. The word "gumbo" is derived from the African term for okra, *gombo*. There are no hard and fast rules for making gumbo beyond the basic roux, okra, and your imagination. I like crawfish gumbo, but you can substitute just about any seafood, such as shrimp, crabs, or scallops.

The most important part of the gumbo is to form a really dark, rich roux. I highly recommend you use a black iron skillet to make your roux.

Ingredients:

- 2 lb crawfish with heads attached (can substitute prawns)
- ½ lb andouille smoked sausage cut in ¾" lengths
- 1 lb lump crabmeat
- 1 large yellow onion, quartered
- 1 large yellow onion, chopped
- 3 cloves garlic, quartered
- 4 cloves of garlic, minced
- 2 stalks of celery, chopped
- 2 stalks of celery split
- 1 green bell pepper, chopped
- 4 medium sized tomatoes, chopped
- 1 lb okra, sliced in ½" lengths
- 8 hot cherry peppers, chopped
- 1 teaspoon fresh thyme
- 3 bay leaves
- 1 cup chicken broth
- ½ cup red wine
- 2 teaspoons Tabasco sauce
- 3 tablespoons tomato paste
- ½ cup canola oil
- ½ cup all-purpose flour
- 2 tablespoons Creole seasoning mix
- Salt & pepper
- 2 cups of cooked white rice

Directions:

Carefully remove the meat from the tail of the crawfish and store in refrigerator for use later. Place remaining heads and shells in large pot with 8 cups of water. Add quartered onion, quartered garlic, and split celery stalks.

Place heat on high and bring to boil, and then reduce to simmer uncovered for at least 2 hours.

Using a colander, separate solids from the stock and discard solids. Return stock to the pot. Add chicken broth as necessary to make at least 6 cups of liquid.

Pre-heat a large heavy pan (preferably a cast iron skillet), on high heat. Add sausage and brown on all sides. Remove sausage and set aside, leaving grease from the sausage in the pan.

Add oil. When oil starts to smoke, carefully add the flour while whisking it into the oil. Continue whisking until the roux turns dark brown (about 6-8 minutes).

Add the chopped onion, chopped celery, bell pepper, minced garlic, and hot cherry peppers. Stir constantly until vegetables are softened and lightly browned (about 3-5 minutes). Add Creole mix, then deglaze with red wine, and reduce heat to simmer.

Bring stock in pot to a boil, and then slowly add the roux mixture with vegetables. Stir thoroughly until all of the roux mixture is absorbed by the stock, and then add the sausage, tomatoes, tomato paste, okra, thyme, bay leaves, tobasco sauce, and salt & pepper to taste.

When Gumbo begins to boil, reduce heat to low and cook for at least one hour.

Add the crawfish tails and lump crabmeat and let simmer for 15 minutes. Season to taste with salt, black pepper, and cayenne pepper. Remove bay leaves.

Serve in a bowl over white rice.

FRENCH ONION SOUP

Onion based soups have been around since the time of the Romans, but the most popular of all onion soups were created in France in the 18th century. The typical French onion soup uses beef broth with caramelized onions and is finished under a broiler with croutons and gruyère melted on top. I prefer to substitute the beef broth with a lighter chicken stock that does not compete with the rich flavor created by the caramelized onions. Caramelization can be accomplished within half an hour, but many chefs allow for hours of cooking to bring out the complex flavors of the onions' sugars. I speed this process up by adding natural sugar to the onion.

Ingredients:
- 4 large red onions, sliced thin
- 4 medium yellow onions, sliced thin
- 2 cloves garlic, minced
- 2 tablespoons Italian parsley, chopped
- 2 bay leaves
- 8 cups chicken stock
- ½ cup dry white wine
- 12 slices baguette, ¼ inch thick
- ¼ teaspoon sugar
- ½ teaspoon thyme
- ½ cup shredded Gruyere cheese
- 3 tablespoons olive oil

Directions:
In large pot on medium heat, add oil and brown onions for 10 minutes. Stir in sugar and cook onions until caramelized (about 30 minutes).

Preheat oven to 350 degrees.

Add the stock, garlic, thyme, bay leaf and wine to pot and bring to boil, then reduce to simmer for about 45 minutes. Salt and pepper to taste.

Using a brush, lightly coat baguette slices with olive oil, then toast in oven (about 5 minutes) and remove.

Set oven to broil.

Remove bay leaves from broth and ladle soup into oven-ready bowls. Place baguette slices on top, sprinkle with heavy layer of cheese.

Set bowls on baking pan under broiler about 4 inches from the heat source. Cook until cheese melts and forms a light brown crust (about 3-4 minutes).

Garnish with a light sprinkle of parsley and serve.

ITALIAN TOMATO PASTA SOUP

The most versatile and probably oldest dish in the world is soup. In fact, the very first restaurants in the world were purveyors of soup. The word "restaurant" is a derivative of the French word for "restore" and was initially used to describe a highly concentrated, inexpensive soup, sold by street vendors in the 16th century. In 1765, a Parisian entrepreneur opened a shop specializing in such soups. This prompted the use of the modern word, "restaurant," to describe shops that sold and served food.

This recipe is true to the tradition of soup that reuses (or restores) leftover marinara sauce. When I make marinara sauce, I typically make a large batch and use the remaining sauce for pizza or a dipping sauce. I use the balance of the marinara sauce to make this richly flavored soup

Ingredients:
- 3 cups marinara sauce (see recipe)
- 1 yellow (sweet) onion, chopped
- 2 cloves garlic, chopped
- 2 carrots, chopped
- 4 cups chicken broth
- 1 lb cannellini beans (Italian kidney beans, can substitute white kidney beans).
- 1 cup small pasta cooked al dente
- 1 teaspoon crushed red pepper
- 1 teaspoon kosher salt
- 2 tablespoons olive oil

Directions:
Put the beans in a large pot and fill with water until the beans are covered with at least 2 inches of water. Bring the beans to a boil over medium heat.

Turn the heat off and let the pot sit until the water cools down. Strain the beans from the soaking water.

In a large pot on high heat, add oil and brown onion for 4-5 minutes. Add garlic and carrots and cook until softened (about 5 minutes).

Add marinara sauce and chicken broth. When soup begins to boil, reduce heat to low and add the beans.

Season with crushed red pepper and salt.

Cook covered for 45 minutes (until beans are soft).

Add pasta and cook for 5-10 minutes until pasta is cooked though and serve.

⋘ LOBSTER BISQUE ⋙

Ingredients:

- 4 lobster tails, diced
- ¼ cup onions, chopped
- ½ cup celery, chopped
- ¼ cup carrots, sliced
- ¼ cup leaks, chopped
- 1/8 cup shallots, chopped
- 3 cups chicken stock
- ½ cup tomato puree
- 2 tablespoons brandy
- ¼ cup white wine
- 1 tablespoon Italian parsley, minced
- 2 teaspoons fresh oregano, minced
- 2 teaspoons fresh thyme, minced
- 1 teaspoon fresh tarragon, minced
- 3 leaves of basil, minced
- 1 bay leaf
- 1 black peppercorn
- ¼ cup heavy cream
- 3 tablespoons butter
- 1/8 cup raw rice
- 1 tablespoon brandy

Directions:

In a large pot over high heat, melt 2 tablespoons butter and then add onions, celery, carrots, and shallots. Cook until vegetables softened (about 5 minutes). Remove vegetables.

Add remaining butter and cook lobster until pink (about 3-5 minutes).

Pour brandy over lobster, cover pan, and cook one minute.

For the next step, it is important to make sure your hood fan is off and have a fully wetted dish cloth nearby. The dish cloth needs to be larger than the pot surface. You will remove the lid, and using a lighter, ignite the brandy soaked lobster. If flames get too large, you can place lid on pot or cover with the wet dish cloth.

When flames disappear, stir in white wine followed, by all of the vegetables and spices. Stir and cook for 3 minutes.

Add chicken stock and 4 cups of water. Turn heat to high and bring to a boil, then reduced to medium to low heat for 30 minutes.

Add tomato purée and cook for 10 minutes.

Using a hand blender, purée the soup in the pot until smooth. Note: Use caution when blending hot liquids.

Bring to a boil, add cream stirring constantly, and serve immediately with a light drizzle of brandy on top of the bisque.

 SPICY BLACK BEAN SOUP

Ingredients:
- 2 cups dried black beans
- ½ white onion, quartered
- 4 large garlic cloves, cut in half
- 4 large fresh sprigs of cilantro
- 2 cans chipotle, chopped
- 6 plump green onions, diced
- 4 cups of chicken broth
- 1 tablespoon fresh pork lard
- 2 teaspoons sea salt
- 1 cup *crema*

Directions:

Place beans in a large pot with 4 cups of hot water and 4 cups of chicken broth. Mix in the onion, garlic, and lard. Bring pot to a boil, then reduce heat, partially cover, and cook until tender (at least 2 hours). Note: Add water as necessary to keep liquid just above the height of the beans.

Turn off the heat and stir in the chipotles. Using a hand blender, purée the beans in the pot, forming a smooth and thick consistency. Note: Use caution when blending hot liquids. Add more water as necessary.

Return heat to medium to low and stir in the cilantro and salt to taste. Stir constantly to prevent sticking. When soup begins to bubble, reduce to simmer for at least 30 minutes, stirring occasionally.

Serve in bowls garnished with crema and diced onions. Recommend serving over rice.

PRIMI DI PASTA
(FIRST COURSE OF PASTA)

ARRABBIATA CARBONARA

ASIAN NOODLES WITH TOMATO SAUCE

BOLOGNESE

KAREN'S CARBONARA

CREAMY PORCINI MUSHROOM PENNE

LEMON SHRIMP IN LINGUINE

LINGUINE WITH CLAM SAUCE

MARINARA ARRABBIATA STYLE

MARINARA SAUCE

MARINARA SAUCE - SOFFRITTO STYLE

PAD THAI

RISOTTO WITH PORCINI MUSHROOMS

SPAGHETTI WITH PORCINI MUSHROOMS & ARUGALA

TOMATO CREAM SAUCE

ARRABBIATA CARBONARA

This dish combines two classic Italian styles of pasta sauce – *Arrabbiata* and *Carbonara*. *Arrabbiata* is a spicy red sauce that dates back to the era of the Romans. *All'arrabbiata* is Italian for "angry style", which stems from the heat of the chili peppers. *Carbonara* typically uses a mixture of cheese, egg yolks, cured fatty pork, and black pepper; however, I do not use raw eggs in this particular dish.

Ingredients:
½ lb pancetta, chopped
1 clove garlic, chopped
1 white onion, diced
2 teaspoons fresh rosemary, chopped
5 fresh basil leaves
1 large can crushed tomatoes
⅓ cup red wine
½ cup pecorino Parmesan
1 tablespoon olive oil
1 teaspoon crushed red pepper flakes
Salt and pepper
1 lb Bucatini pasta

Directions:
In a pre-heated pan on high heat, add olive oil and brown the pancetta for 3-5 minutes.

Add onion and cook until golden brown (approximately 3-5 minutes), then add the garlic, rosemary, and red pepper flakes. Cook for 3 minutes, then deglaze with red wine. Cook until wine is reduced.

Stir in tomatoes, salt, and pepper. Cook on medium heat for 10 minutes.

Add basil and reduce heat to simmer; cook for 15 minutes or until thickened. Toss with cooked bucatini and pecorino Parmesan.

ASIAN NOODLES WITH TOMATO SAUCE

Ingredients:
- 12 oz medium thick dried noodles
- 4 tablespoons olive oil
- 2 garlic cloves, minced
- 4 shallots, chopped
- 2 carrots, diced
- 4 oz button mushrooms, quartered
- 2 oz peas (fresh)
- 1 tablespoon tomato ketchup (see recipe)
- 2 teaspoons tomato paste
- ½ teaspoon chili powder
- 1 teaspoon paprika
- ¼ cup red wine
- Salt & pepper
- ¼ stick butter

Directions:
Cook noodles in boiling water until just tender, then remove and rinse immediately with cold water. To keep noodles from sticking together, mix noodles with one tablespoon of olive oil and set aside.

In pre-heated wok, heat oil and add garlic, shallots, and carrots. Cook until softened (about 3-4 minutes). Then add mushrooms, peas, chili powder, and paprika. Stir fry for 3-4 minutes more.

Deglaze pan with wine and cook until reduced (about 3 minutes).

Stir in tomato ketchup and paste, and cook until sauce slightly reduces (about 3 minutes).

Reduce heat to medium and gently stir in noodles. Cook over a medium heat until noodles are fully cooked and have taken on the reddish tinge of the paprika and tomato (about 5-6 minutes).

BOLOGNESE

Bolognese sauce is a meat-based sauce for pasta originating in Bologna, Italy. This is a variation of a traditional Bolognese sauce that uses hot cherry peppers to spice it up. Be careful when adding salt to this dish, since both the pancetta and meat stock have a lot of salt in them. Also, you may not need as much olive oil depending on the fat content of the pancetta.

Ingredients:
* ½ lb of Beef shoulder, chopped
* Pork ¼ lb
* Pancetta ¼ lb
* 3 cloves garlic, sliced
* 1 yellow onion, diced
* 1 celery stalk, diced
* 1 carrot, diced
* 3 cloves garlic, minced
* 4 hot cherry peppers, sliced
* 1 fresh rosemary sprig
* 1 fresh thyme sprig
* 2 flat leaf parsley sprigs
* ½ cup red wine
* 1 ½ cups chicken stock
* 3 tablespoons tomato paste (1 small can)
* 2 tablespoons flour

- 2 tablespoons olive oil
- Cheese cloth
- Pasta (recommend wide flat pasta such as Pappardelle)

Directions:

In pre-heated pan on high heat, thoroughly brown meat, and then scrape into a bowl.

In the same pan on medium to high heat, add olive oil and cook garlic until golden brown, then discard it. Then use the garlic infused oil in the same pan to brown pancetta for 5 minutes. Add onion, celery, and carrot, then sauté until onion is golden brown. Deglaze with red wine and cook until wine is reduced (about 3 minutes).

Stir in 2 tablespoons flour and cook for 2 minutes before next step.

Add meat, peppers, and stock; bring to boil, let simmer, and season with salt and pepper to taste.

Create a "bouquet garni" with the cheese cloth by rolling together 1 fresh rosemary sprig, 1 fresh thyme sprig, and 2 flat leaf parsley sprigs. Tie the ends with string or strips of the cheese cloth. Place bouquet garni in the sauce.

Simmer and keep covered for up to 3 hours.

Stir in tomato paste and cook for an additional 45 minutes.

Mix with pasta and serve with shaved Parmesan garnish.

KAREN'S CARBONARA

Recipes for Carbonara vary, though most use the basic ingredients of cheese, raw egg yolks, cured fatty pork, and black pepper. These ingredients are combined with the heat of the hot pasta to cook the eggs. Be sure to serve this classic meal on preheated dishes to keep it warm longer. Note, however, that many health professionals advise against serving eggs that are not fully cooked to infants, the elderly, or anyone with a compromised immune system.

Karen created this particular version to make it healthier by using fewer fats (creams and cheese) and less eggs, but if you want a more authentic version, you can substitute fat free half and half with heavy cream, double the eggs, and add more cheese.

Ingredients:
- ½ pound pancetta, coarsely chopped
- 1 medium yellow onion chopped
- 2 tablespoons fresh flat-leaf parsley, minced
- 2 garlic cloves, minced
- 2 egg yolks
- ½ cup fat free half and half
- 1 teaspoon coarsely cracked pepper
- ½ teaspoon salt
- ¾ cup grated Parmesan cheese
- 1 tablespoon olive oil
- 1 lb dried spaghetti (recommend Bucatini)

Directions:
Bring a large pot of salted water to a boil over high heat. Add the pasta, stir well and cook until al dente (tender but firm to the bite) (about 10 minutes).

In a large bowl, combine the egg yolks, Parmesan cheese, half and half, parsley, and pepper. Whisk thoroughly.

While the pasta is cooking, pre-heat a pan on medium to high heat and add the olive oil. When the oil is hot, add the onion and garlic, stir until the onion and garlic softens.. Add the pancetta and cook until it is slightly brown..

Using tongs, transfer the pasta, still wet, to the bowl with the egg mixture and add in the pancetta and onion mix. Toss immediately to coat pasta.

Garnish with minced parsley.

Serve immediately on warmed dishes.

CREAMY PORCINI MUSHROOM PENNE

This is a creamy variation of my Spaghetti with Porcini Mushrooms that incorporates Italian cheeses. As before, you can use any mushroom in this dish, but I prefer the porcini mushroom. If you use a dried mushroom, cook mushrooms in 2 cups of chicken broth for 20 minutes, then drain off and reserve the stock for later use.

Ingredients:
- 1 cup porcini mushrooms, sliced
- 2 shallots, diced
- 2 cloves garlic, minced
- 2 tablespoons chopped chives
- ½ cup Mascarpone cheese
- ½ cup white wine
- ¼ cup chicken stock
- ½ cup Parmesan cheese
- 2 tablespoons olive oil
- Salt and pepper
- 1 lb penne pasta

Directions:

In pre-heated pan on medium to high heat, add olive oil and brown shallots and garlic (about 3-5 minutes). Then add mushrooms and cook an additional 3-5 minutes.

Deglaze with white wine and cook until wine is reduced (about 3 minutes). Then add chicken stock (or stock reserved from boiling dried mushrooms) and cook 5-10 minutes. Salt and pepper to taste.

Bring a large pot three-fourths full of salted water to a boil over high heat. Add the pasta, stir well, and cook until al dente (tender but firm to the bite), about 10 minutes.

In a large bowl, mix sauce with Mascarpone cheese, then stir in the pasta.

Add Parmesan and garnish with chives.

LEMON SHRIMP IN LINGUINE

Ingredients:
- 1 lb shrimp, peeled and deveined
- Zest of 2 lemons
- Juice of 1 lemon
- ½ cup Italian parsley, chopped
- ½ cup arugula sliced thin
- 2 shallots, chopped
- 2 cloves garlic, minced
- ⅓ cup olive oil
- Salt and pepper
- 1 lb linguine

Directions:

In a preheated pan on medium heat, prepare lemon infused olive oil by mixing ¼ cup of the olive oil and the zest of one lemon. Cook for 3 minutes and set aside for future use.

Bring a large pot three-fourths full of salted water to a boil over high heat. Add the pasta, stir well, and cook until al dente (tender but firm to the bite), about 10 minutes.

In the same pan on medium to high heat, add 2 tablespoons olive oil and brown shallots and garlic (about 3-5 minutes).

Add shrimp and stir fry for 3-5 minutes, and then add zest and juice of one lemon.

In a large bowl, add the linguine and pour in the shrimp with sauce. Add parsley and arugula and mix in lemon infused oil. Salt and pepper to taste.

LINGUINE WITH CLAM SAUCE

Ingredients:
- 2 lb clams in shells
- 4 cloves garlic, thinly sliced
- Juice of 1 lemon
- ½ cup dry white wine
- ½ cup chicken broth
- 1 teaspoon crushed red pepper flakes
- Handful of coarsely chopped Italian parsley
- Kosher salt & pepper
- ¼ cup olive oil
- 1 lb linguine

Directions:
Bring a large pot three-fourths full of salted water to a boil over high heat. Add the pasta, stir well, and cook until al dente (tender but firm

to the bite), about 10 minutes.

In pre-heated pan over medium heat, add clams with wine. As clams begin to open, pull them out and place in a bowl. After 3 minutes, discard any clams that do not open.

Strain clam broth with cheese cloth and reserve for later use.

Over medium to high heat, warm olive oil in a pan and sauté the garlic until golden brown (about 3 minutes), then add reserved clam broth, chicken broth, and lemon juice. Simmer for 3-5 min, then add red pepper flakes, salt & pepper.

Thoroughly drain linguine and mix into pan; then add the clams. Cook over low heat for 1-2 minutes.

Toss with parsley and serve.

 ## MARINARA ARRABBIATA STYLE

Arrabbiata is a spicy red sauce that dates back to the era of the Romans. All'arrabbiata is Italian for "angry style", which stems from the heat of the chili peppers. This dish is usually served with pasta and chopped fresh parsley sprinkled on top.

Ingredients:
- 1 clove garlic, chopped
- 1 lb cherry tomatoes, sliced in half
- 1 teaspoon fresh rosemary, chopped
- 5 fresh basil leaves, sliced thin
- 1 large can crushed tomatoes
- ⅓ cup red wine
- 2 tablespoons olive oil

- 1 teaspoon crushed red pepper flakes
- Salt and pepper
- 1 pound penne pasta or rigatoni

Directions:
In pre-heated pan on medium to high heat, add olive oil and crushed red pepper. Then sauté garlic and rosemary for 5 minutes.

Deglaze with red wine and cook until reduced (about 3 minutes).

Add crushed tomatoes, salt and pepper. Cook on medium-low heat for at least 20 minutes.

Add cherry tomatoes and basil. Reduce heat and cook for 10 minutes or until thickened. Toss with cooked pasta.

MARINARA SAUCE

This is the staple of many great Italian dishes. Marinara sauce originated in Naples after the Spaniards introduced the tomato from the New World. The word "marinara" is derived from "marinaro", which is Italian for "of the sea". It is a very versatile tomato-based sauce that you can use for pizza, pasta, meatballs, and soups. There are many versions of this sauce; however, the most common ingredients are tomatoes, onions, and basil. Many chefs also add garlic.

Ingredients:
- 1 28 oz can Italian plum tomatoes
- 1 16 oz can tomato sauce
- 6 basil leaves
- ½ yellow onion, minced
- 1 teaspoon fresh thyme, minced

- ¼ cup red wine
- 1 cup chicken broth
- 2 tablespoons olive oil
- Pinch dry oregano
- Salt and pepper

Directions:
In a pre-heated pan on medium to high heat, add olive oil and sauté onions until soft (about 3-5 minutes). Add oregano and thyme.

Deglaze pan with red wine and cook until reduced (about 3 minutes).

Stir in plum tomatoes, tomato sauce, and chicken broth.

Raise heat until sauce begins to boil, then reduce heat and simmer for 30 minutes. Salt and pepper to taste.

Stir in basil and cook an additional 10 minutes on simmer.

MARINARA SAUCE - SOFFRITTO STYLE

"Sofritto" is the Italian word for "sub-fried" or "under-fried" that refers to using a small quantity of olive oil to cook diced vegetables that constitute the base of the dish. In Southern Italy, the soffritto is generally prepared with olive oil, chopped onions, and diced garlic. In Northern Italy, the soffritto is made with the "holy trinity" of Italian vegetables - minced celery, carrot, and onion. The addition of these ingredients creates a much more robust and flavorful dish.

Ingredients:
- 1 28 oz can Italian plum tomatoes
- 1 16 oz can tomato sauce
- ½ yellow onion, minced
- 1 carrot, chopped

- 1 celery stalk, chopped
- 1 clove garlic, minced
- 1 teaspoon fresh thyme, minced
- 2 bay leaves
- ¼ cup red wine
- 1 cup chicken broth
- 2 tablespoons olive oil
- Pinch dry oregano
- Salt and pepper

Directions:

In a pre-heated pan on medium to high heat, add olive oil and sauté onions, celery, and carrots until soft (about 3-5 minutes). Add garlic, oregano, and thyme and cook 3 minutes.

Deglaze pan with red wine and cook until reduced (about 3 minutes).

Stir in plum tomatoes, tomato sauce, chicken broth, and bay leaves.

Raise heat until sauce begins to boil, then reduce heat and simmer for one hour. Salt and pepper to taste.

Remove bay leaves prior to serving.

 PAD THAI

Pad Thai is one of Thailand's national dishes, and consists of stir-fried rice noodles with a variety of fresh vegetables, fish sauce, and tamarind.

Ingredients:
- 2 dozen fresh jumbo shrimp, peeled and deveined
- 1 lb rice noodles
- ¼ cup tamarind sauce

- ½ cup orange juice
- 2 tablespoons honey
- 2 tablespoons rice vinegar
- 3 oz soy sauce
- 2 tablespoons chili paste
- 2 tablespoons brown sugar
- 1 tablespoon oyster sauce
- 3 tablespoons sesame oil
- ¼ cup cilantro, chopped
- 1 cup fresh bean sprouts
- Garlic chives

Directions:
Soak rice noodles in cold water for 45 minutes to one hour. Make sure that the noodles are soft on the outside, yet firm on the inside (al dente).

In a bowl, create the tamarind glaze by mixing the tamarind sauce, orange juice, honey, and rice vinegar.

In pre-heated wok on medium to high heat, add a tablespoon of sesame oil and sauté shrimp for 2 minutes; then remove and place shrimp in a bowl and toss with ¼ cup of the tamarind glaze.

Create the sauce by mixing the remaining tamarind glaze with soy sauce, chili paste, brown sugar, and oyster sauce.

With heat on high, add remaining sesame oil to the wok, then garlic chives. Cook 2-3 minutes, then add the sauce and cilantro. Add noodles to wok and toss thoroughly with the sauce for 2-3 minutes.

Mix in shrimp with glaze and cook until reduced (about 3-4 minutes).

Reduce heat to medium and stir in bean sprouts. Cook 2-3 minutes and serve.

Note: If noodles are too firm, stir a little chicken broth into the noodles and let the juices cook in.

RISOTTO WITH PORCINI MUSHROOMS

Ingredients:
- 1 cup dried porcini mushrooms
- ½ onion, chopped
- 3 celery sticks, diced
- 2 tablespoons Italian parsley, minced
- 1 ½ cups Arborio rice
- ½ cup white wine
- 2 cups chicken broth
- 3 handfuls freshly grated Parmesan cheese
- ¼ stick butter
- 2 tablespoons olive oil
- Salt & pepper

Directions:
In a pot on medium heat, simmer dried porcini mushrooms in chicken stock for 20 minutes. Drain mushrooms and reserve broth for later use.

In a pre-heated pan on high heat, add olive oil. Then add onion, celery, salt & pepper. Cook until vegetables are softened (about 4-5 minutes).

Mix mushroom into onions. Cook 3-5 minutes.

Stir in 1 ½ cups of Arborio rice. Continue stirring until rice toasts. When rice is properly toasted, you will notice a golden brown spot start to form in each rice kernel. This will take at least 10 minutes.

Add ½ cup white wine and cook until reduced (about 3 minutes).

Ladle in enough chicken broth to barely cover the rice. Cover and cook for 20-30 minutes, stirring occasionally. Keep adding more broth until rice is firm but ready to eat.

Uncover and mix in butter, parsley, and grated Parmesan cheese. Turn off heat and let sit for 3-5 minutes before serving.

⟶ SPAGHETTI WITH ⟵
PORCINI MUSHROOMS & ARUGALA

You can use any mushroom in this dish, but I prefer the porcini mushroom. If you use dried mushrooms, reconstitute them by cooking the dried mushrooms in 2 cups of chicken broth for 20 minutes, then drain off and reserve the stock for later use.

Ingredients:
- 1 cup porcini mushrooms, sliced
- 1 cup arugula, chopped
- 2 shallots, diced
- 2 cloves garlic, minced
- 2 tablespoons chopped chives
- 2 tablespoons capers
- ½ cup white wine
- ¼ cup chicken stock
- 2 tablespoons olive oil
- 1 pinch crushed red pepper
- Salt and pepper
- 1 lb penne pasta

Directions:
In a pre-heated pan on medium to high heat, add olive oil with

crushed red pepper, then brown the shallots and garlic (about 3-5 minutes). Then add mushrooms, arugula, and capers. Cook an additional 3-5 minutes.

Deglaze with white wine and cook until wine is reduced (about 3 minutes). Then add chicken stock (or stock reserved from boiling dried mushrooms) and cook 5-10 minutes or until sauce is reduced and thickened. Salt and pepper to taste.

Bring a large pot three-fourths full of salted water to a boil over high heat. Add the pasta, stir well, and cook until al dente (tender but firm to the bite), about 10 minutes.

In a large bowl, thoroughly mix sauce into pasta. Garnish with chives and serve.

TOMATO CREAM SAUCE

This is a healthy version of a traditional tomato cream sauce that substitutes cream with low fat yogurt.

Ingredients:
- 1 28 oz can Italian plum tomatoes
- 1 16 oz can tomato sauce
- 6 basil leaves
- ½ yellow onion, minced
- 1 teaspoon fresh thyme, minced
- ¼ cup red wine
- 1 cup chicken broth
- 1 cup low fat vanilla yogurt
- 2 tablespoons olive oil
- Pinch dry oregano
- Salt and pepper

Directions:

In pre-heated pan on medium to high heat, add olive oil and sauté onions until soft (about 3-5 minutes). Add oregano and thyme.

Deglaze pan with red wine and cook until reduced (about 3 minutes).

Stir in plum tomatoes, tomato sauce, and chicken broth.

Raise heat until sauce begins to boil, then reduce heat and simmer for one hour. Salt and pepper to taste.

Stir in basil, then one cup low fat vanilla yogurt. Using hand blender, purée the sauce in the pot into a smooth consistency. Note: Use caution when blending hot liquids.

Cook 15 minutes on simmer.

SECONDI DI CARNI E VOLATILI
(SECOND COURSES OF MEATS AND CHICKEN)

BEEF FAJITAS
BRAISED LAMB IN MEDITERRANEAN TOMATO SAUCE
CHICKEN ENCHILADAS WITH RED SALSA
CHICKEN ENCHILADAS WITH SPICY CHORIZO
CHICKEN SCALOPPINI WITH SAFFRON SAUCE
COQ AU VIN BLANCO
COQ AU VIN ROUGE
CORNISH HENS WITH SPICY GARLIC SALSA
GRILLED LEMON GARLIC LAMB CHOPS
GRILLED SAUSAGE WITH ONIONS & PEPPERS
ITALIAN MEATBALLS
ITALIAN MEATLOAF WITH JALAPEÑO BALSAMIC GLAZE
MAPLE BRAISED BEEF SHORT RIBS
MEAT TACOS
MONGOLIAN BBQ RIBS
RACK OF LAMB
ROAST BEEF WITH SPICY ITALIAN TOMATO SAUCE
ROASTED TURKEY
ROTISSERIE LEMON AND HERB CHICKEN
SOUTHERN FRIED CHICKEN
SMOKED BABY BACK RIBS
SPICE RUBBED PORK TENDERLOIN
TAMARIND GLAZED CHICKEN
TANDOORI CHICKEN
TUSCAN PORK CHOPS
VEAL LEMON
VEAL OSSO BUCO IN TOMATO SAUCE
VEAL PARMIGIANA

BEEF FAJITAS

Ingredients:
- 1-2 lbs beef round cut in 2-3 in strips
- 5 cloves garlic
- ½ habanero pepper
- ¼ cup cilantro
- 1 tablespoon taco seasoning mix (see recipe)
- 8 corn tortillas
- 1 red bell pepper, sliced in thin strips
- 1 green bell pepper, sliced in thin strips
- 1 yellow onion, sliced in thin strips
- 1 tablespoon olive oil
- Salt & pepper

Directions:
In a food processor, mix garlic, cilantro, and habanero pepper until minced.

In mixing bowl, mix meat with garlic/cilantro mix, taco seasoning, olive oil, salt & pepper. Mix thoroughly and transfer to a plastic storage bag, seal, and let stand for at least 1 hour.

In pre-heated pan, add olive oil and heat until very hot. Add meat and stir occasionally until meat is browned on all sides (approximately 5 minutes). Then add peppers and onion and stir fry until vegetables are lightly browned, yet still crisp.

Pre-heat tortillas as follows: Pre-heat oven to 350 degrees. Spread a slightly damp paper towel or napkins on a baking sheet, and then cover with the tortillas. Add another layer of slightly damp paper towel or napkins. Bake for 5-10 minutes.

BRAISED LAMB IN MEDITERRANEAN TOMATO SAUCE

This is an "Osso Buco" style of cooking braised lamb in a rich sauce of tomato and dried fruit. Recommend serving with cous cous.

Ingredients:
- 6 lamb shanks
- 1 yellow onion, diced
- 1 carrot, diced
- 2 stalks celery, diced
- 3 cloves fresh garlic, minced
- 4 tomatoes, diced
- 8 oz moist pitted prunes, cut in quarters
- 3 tablespoons diced fresh basil
- 2 tablespoons chopped fresh thyme
- 1 ½ cups red wine
- 4-6 cups chicken stock
- 3 ounces tomato paste
- 1 cup flour
- 3 tablespoons olive oil
- Salt, pepper and, paprika

Directions:
Rub lamb with salt, pepper, and paprika; let stand for one hour at room temp.

Pre-heat oven to 325 degrees.

Coat lamb with sifted flour.

In large pre-heated pan, add olive oil and brown lamb on all sides (about 2-3 minutes per side). Then remove and set in large roasting pan with cover (Dutch oven) with bones facing up.

In the same pan, brown the onion, celery, carrots, basil, and thyme. When vegetables are softened, add garlic and cook for an additional 2 minutes. Then add red wine to deglaze the pan. Let wine cook down until reduced. Stir in meat stock, prunes, tomatoes, and paste. Add Salt and pepper.

Pour broth mix over top of the shanks.

Let cook covered in oven for at least 2-3 hours.

Transfer lamb to serving platter, cover with aluminum foil, and let stand in warming drawer or oven at 180 degrees.

Skim the fat off the top of the sauce in the roasting pan.

Place roasting pan on stove over medium heat and cook down until a thick sauce remains (approximately 30 minutes). Season to taste.

Serve over cous cous.

CHICKEN ENCHILADAS WITH RED SALSA

Ingredients:
- 2 cups shredded chicken white meat
- 10 ancho chilies (dried poblanos)
- 1 can diced tomatoes with juice
- ½ white onion, coarsely chopped
- Small white onion, sliced into thin rings
- 6 cloves garlic
- 1 teaspoon oregano
- 1 ½ cups chicken stock
- 4 tablespoons canola or safflower oil

- Sea salt
- 12 white corn tortillas (6 in)
- ½ cup crema

Directions for the red salsa:
Tear ancho chilies into large pieces, then place in a bowl and add boiling water to cover (you can weigh the chilies down with a plate). Let soak 15 min until soft. Drain, then blend until smooth in food processor with tomatoes with juice, chopped onion, garlic, and oregano. Add chicken stock as necessary, to create smooth consistency.

Heat 1 tablespoon oil in a pan and add sauce. Cook until thickened, adding remaining chicken stock and cook 5 min. Add sea salt to taste. Lower heat to simmer.

Pre-heat oven to 350 degrees.

Directions for the tortillas:
In a frying pan, heat 3 tablespoons oil until sizzling hot. Quickly swipe tortillas through oil, then pat dry with paper towels.

In a pan, heat oil, then add chopped garlic, then shredded chicken. Stir fry for 5 min and add enough of the sauce to thoroughly coat the chicken.

Directions to complete:
In a baking dish, spread thin layer of sauce. Roll chicken mix in tortillas and line up in dish. Spoon remaining sauce over top and bake for 10 min. Serve with fresh onion slices and crema. Place slices of jalapeños on top for added spice.

ᏯᏫ CHICKEN ENCHILADAS ᏬᏬ WITH SPICY CHORIZO

Ingredients:
- 4 pieces of chicken with skin and bones intact
- ½ white onion, cut in quarters
- ½ white onion, minced
- 2 cloves garlic, smashed
- 2 cloves garlic, minced
- 1 teaspoon sea salt
- 1 tablespoon canola or safflower oil
- ½ lb Mexican chorizo, casing removed & crumbled
- 1 14 oz can chopped tomatoes, drained
- 1 teaspoon oregano
- 2 bay leaves
- 2 cans chipotles
- 6 soft tortilla shells

Directions:
Place chicken, onion quarters, 1 teaspoon sea salt, and smashed garlic in saucepan; cover with water and bring to a boil. Skim off any foam. Reduce heat and simmer uncovered for 30 min.

Remove meat from chicken, discarding skin and bones. Shred meat by hand and reserve broth.

Place large pan with a lid (Dutch oven) over high flame, add oil, and fry chorizo for 5 minutes.

Reserve one tablespoon of the excess grease from the pan and drain off the rest.

Add diced onions & garlic. Brown for 2-3 minutes.

Add chicken, tomatoes, oregano, bay leaves, chipotles, 1 tablespoon of chipotle sauce and 1 cup of the broth. Simmer uncovered for 15 minutes until reduced. Add broth as necessary, to maintain thick consistency.

Remove bay leaves and salt to taste.

Pre-heat oven to 350 degrees.

Roll tortillas with chicken mix and place in baking dish, reserving some of the sauce. Spoon the reserved sauce from the chicken mix over the top of the enchiladas. Cover with foil and bake for 10 minutes.

CHICKEN SCALOPPINI WITH SAFFRON SAUCE

Ingredients:
- 6 Boneless chicken breasts
- 2 shallots, sliced thin
- 1 clove garlic, diced
- 1 ½ cups chicken broth
- 1 ½ pinches saffron
- ½ cup white wine
- ½ cup cream (can substitute half and half)
- ¼ cup Italian parsley, chopped
- Salt and pepper
- Olive oil

Directions:
Using a meat hammer, place wax paper or plastic wrap over chicken and pound out chicken until flattened. Salt and pepper chicken.

In pre-heated pan over medium to high heat, add olive oil and brown chicken on both sides for 3 minutes. Set aside.

In the same pan, add more oil if necessary and brown shallots and garlic for 2-3 minutes; add salt and pepper. Deglaze with white wine and let cook until wine is reduced (approximately 3-5 minutes).

Add chicken broth and saffron. Cook until reduced (10-15 minutes).

Add cream, then place chicken in mix and cook until thickened (about 5-10 minutes).

Sprinkle with fresh parsley and serve over pasta.

 Coq Au Vin Blanc

Most people are familiar with the red-wine cousin of this dish. This is a dish that I invented to bring together the cooking style of the county-French classic, Coq Au Vin, with the Italian-style chicken scaloppini. White wine is used in place of red wine and lemon; capers are added to create a very unique dish. I prefer to use a Chardonnay or Sauvignon Blanc for the wine.

Ingredients:
- Whole roaster chicken, cut into pieces
- 6 slices thick bacon
- 3 cloves garlic, minced
- ½ lb white button mushrooms (quartered)
- 10 oz frozen baby or pearl onions
- 2 tablespoons Italian parsley, chopped
- 1 lemon, sliced
- 2 tablespoons capers
- 1 cup flour
- ¼ cup brandy

- 1 bottle dry white wine
- 4 cups chicken broth
- Salt and pepper
- Pinch of cayenne pepper
- 3 tablespoons olive oil

Directions:
Cut chicken into pieces and rub with fresh garlic, ground pepper, and sea salt. Then place in food storage bag with entire bottle of white wine. Set bag on a large bowl and place in refrigerator overnight.

In a large pan on high heat, cook bacon until crispy, extracting all grease. Remove bacon and reserve all but 1 tablespoon of fat for frying the chicken. Save remaining oil to add as necessary.

Salt and pepper chicken, then roll in flour.

Add one tablespoon of olive oil to heated pan with bacon grease.

Brown the chicken on all sides until golden brown. As you add and remove chicken pieces, add equal parts of bacon grease and olive oil to keep pan fully coated with grease.

Place all chicken in large pot with lid (Dutch oven), starting with the dark meat (thighs and legs) on the bottom. Set pot on stove with high heat. After 5 minutes, pour brandy over chicken, cover pan, and cook one minute.

For the next step it is important to make sure your hood fan is off and have a soaking wet dish cloth near by. The dish cloth needs to be larger than the pot surface. You will remove the lid, and using a lighter, ignite the brandy soaked chicken. If flames get too large, you can place lid on pot or cover with wet dish cloth.

When flames disappear, add left over wine from marinade, chicken broth, lemon slices, and garlic to the pot; cover and cook for one hour.

In a separate pan, use the remaining bacon fat to brown the mushrooms (3-5 minutes). Add onions and cook for 2-3 minutes. Then add parsley, capers, and a pinch of cayenne pepper; mix thoroughly.

Pour mushroom and onion mix into pot with chicken; remove lid and cook for 20 minutes until sauce thickens.

⊂∞ COQ AU VIN ROUGE ∞⊃

This recipe is for those of you that prefer the traditional red wine version of this classic dish. I prefer to use a more fruit-forward wine, such as a merlot, shiraz, or a red zinfandel.

Ingredients:
- Whole roaster chicken, cut into pieces
- 6 slices thick bacon
- 3 cloves garlic, minced
- ½ lb white button mushrooms (quartered)
- 10 oz frozen baby or pearl onions
- 2 tablespoons Italian parsley, chopped
- 1 tablespoon tomato paste
- 1 cup flour
- ¼ cup brandy
- 1 bottle dry red wine
- 4 cups chicken broth
- Salt and pepper
- 1 teaspoon crushed red pepper
- 3 tablespoons olive oil

Directions:

Cut chicken into pieces and rub with fresh garlic, ground pepper, and sea salt. Then put in food storage bag with entire bottle of red wine. Set bag in a large bowl and place in refrigerator overnight.

In a large pan on high heat, cook bacon until crispy, extracting all grease. Remove bacon and reserve all but 1 tablespoon of fat for frying the chicken. Save remaining oil to add as necessary.

Salt and pepper chicken, then roll in flour.

Add one tablespoon of olive oil to heated pan with bacon grease.

Brown the chicken on all sides until golden brown. As you add and remove chicken pieces, add equal parts of bacon grease and olive oil to keep pan fully coated with grease.

Place all chicken in a large pot with lid (Dutch oven), starting with the dark meat (thighs and legs) on the bottom. Set pot on stove with high heat. After 5 minutes, pour brandy over chicken, cover pan, and cook one minute.

For the next step, it is important to make sure your hood fan is off and have a soaking wet dish cloth nearby. The dish cloth needs to be larger than the pot surface. You will remove the lid, and using a lighter, ignite the brandy soaked chicken. If flames get too large, you can place lid on pot or cover with wet dish cloth.

When flames disappear, add left over wine from marinade, chicken broth, and garlic to the pot; cover and cook for one hour.

In a separate pan, use the remaining bacon fat to brown the mushrooms (3-5 minutes). Add onions and cook for 2-3 minutes. Then add parsley and 1 teaspoon of crushed pepper and mix thoroughly.

Pour mushroom and onion mix into pot with chicken, add tomato paste, remove lid, and cook for 20 minutes until sauce thickens.

⊂⊂ CORNISH HENS ⊃⊃
WITH SPICY GARLIC SALSA

Ingredients:
- 6 Cornish hens, cut into quarters
- 4 Serrano chilies
- Juice from 3 limes
- 1 lime, sliced thinly
- ¼ cup red wine vinegar
- ¼ cup Dijon mustard
- ¼ cup honey
- 4 cloves garlic
- ½ cup of cilantro, minced
- 8 cilantro sprigs
- ½ cup olive oil
- Salt & pepper
- ½ cup crumbled white Monterey Jack cheese

Directions:

In a food processor, create salsa mix using the Serrano chilies, lime juice, red wine vinegar, Dijon mustard, honey, garlic, minced cilantro, and olive oil. Blend thoroughly.

Place hens in a large storage bad and pour salsa mix over top. Place in refrigerator overnight.

Remove hens and pour remaining salsa mix into a pot. Cook mix for 10-15 minutes until it slightly thickens.

Grill hens 8-10 minutes on each side.

Serve each hen with a tablespoon of salsa, sprinkle with crumbled cheese, and garnish with limes and cilantro sprigs.

❧ GRILLED LEMON GARLIC LAMB CHOPS ☙

Ingredients:
- 16 lamb loin chops (4 oz each), trim fat off
- 2 tablespoons olive oil
- 2 tablespoons fresh lemon juice
- 1 teaspoon lemon zest
- 1 tablespoon oregano
- 3 cloves minced garlic
- 3/4 teaspoon salt
- 1/2 teaspoon pepper

Directions:
Rub lamb with salt, pepper, oregano, lemon zest, and garlic; then place in zip lock with lemon juice and remaining oregano. Let stand at room temp for up to 1 hour.

Grill for 4-5 minutes per side

❧ GRILLED SAUSAGE WITH ONIONS & PEPPERS ☙

Ingredients:
- 8 links fresh Italian sausage
- 2 red bell peppers, sliced thin
- 1 sweet yellow onion, sliced thin
- 1 cup sweet Marsala wine
- 1/2 cup chicken broth

- 2 tablespoons olive oil
- 1 teaspoon crushed red pepper
- Kosher salt

Directions:

In pre-heated pan on high heat, brown sausage thoroughly on all sides.

Set aside sausage on paper towels. Drain off excess grease from the pan.

In the same pan, add the olive oil and brown onions until softened (approximately 3-5 minutes); then add peppers and crushed red pepper. Cook an additional 3 minutes.

Add sausage back into pan. Then add Marsala wine to deglaze the pan. Cook until wine is reduced (approximately 3-5 minutes).

Then add chicken stock and cook until completely reduced. Add salt and pepper to taste.

 ITALIAN MEATBALLS

Italians traditionally do not serve their meatballs over pasta such as the American version of "Spaghetti and Meatballs." This is a traditional Italian style meatball that is slow cooked in Marinara sauce. You can serve this as either a main course or an appetizer.

Ingredients:

- ½ lb ground beef
- ½ lb ground veal
- ¼ lb ground pork
- ½ cup Italian parsley, minced

- ½ tablespoon Oregano
- 2 tablespoons dry vermouth
- Grated zest of 2 lemons
- 2 cups soft, white bread crumbs
- 2 eggs
- 2 garlic cloves, minced
- 1 teaspoon kosher salt
- 1 teaspoon fresh ground pepper
- 6 cups of marinara sauce (see recipe)

Directions:
In deep pot, prepare a Marinara sauce (see recipe).

In a large bowl, mix all ingredients and form balls approximately 2 inches in diameter.

Place meatballs in sauce, cover and cook for 40 minutes.

Remove lid and cook for an additional 20 minutes until sauce is reduced, skimming off any excess grease.

ITALIAN MEATLOAF WITH JALAPEÑO BALSAMIC GLAZE

This dish is a fusion of my Italian meatballs and a spicy Jalapeño reduction sauce that I created for my wife, Karen, who likes everything spicy. This is also the favorite dish of my daughter-in-law, Nicole, who is a vegetarian. For Nicole's dish, I replace the ground meat with two cups of well cooked black beans and ½ cup of rolled oats (not instant). It is another dish that is great for entertaining because you can prep it early and it will keep well in a warming drawer or an oven with low temperature.

Ingredients:
- ½ lb ground beef
- ½ lb ground veal
- ¼ lb ground pork
- 2 cups soft, white bread crumbs
- 2 eggs
- 2 garlic cloves
- 1 large onion, diced
- ¼ cup dry vermouth
- Handful of flat-leaf parsley, minced
- ½ lb mushrooms, diced
- Grated zest of 2 lemons
- 1 cup heavy cream
- 1 ½ teaspoons fresh oregano
- 1 ½ teaspoons minced fresh thyme
- Sea salt and pepper to taste
- ¾ lb apple wood smoked bacon
- 1 cup Jalapeño Balsamic wine reduction for basting (see recipe)
- 2 tablespoons olive oil

Directions:
Pre-heat oven to 400 degrees.

In a large pre-heated pan over medium to high heat, add olive oil. Then add onions and sauté until brown (about 3-5 minutes), then add mushrooms and garlic. Cook 5 additional minutes. Deglaze with vermouth and cook until wine reduces (about 2-3 minutes).

Stir in cream, parsley, oregano, thyme, and lemon zest. Cook 5 minutes.

In a large bowl, mix in meats, bread crumbs, eggs, and add the onion and mushroom sauce.

Take a bread-sized baking pan and line bottom and sides with bacon, allowing bacon to overlap edges enough to cover loaf. Add meat mixture and fold bacon ends over the mixture to enclose it completely. Cover pan with aluminum foil.

Set pan in a larger roasting pan full of boiling water, then cover roasting pan with foil.

Bake in oven for 1 hour, then remove foil and coat meat with the Jalapeño Balsamic Wine reduction sauce. Return pan and cook 30 additional minutes.

Remove and let stand for at least 10 minutes.

Carefully remove loaf and coat with remaining Jalapeño Balsamic reduction. Slice and serve with caramelized onions and mashed potatoes.

MAPLE BRAISED BEEF SHORT RIBS

This is one of my favorite dishes. I took the classic version of this dish and introduced hot cherry peppers and fresh ginger to balance the sugars of the maple syrup. It is also the perfect dish for entertaining because you can prepare it, place it in the oven, and not have to do too much after your guests arrive.

Ingredients:
- 12 beef short ribs cut in 1"-2" lengths
- 1 carrot, chopped
- 1 onion, chopped
- 2 stalks celery, chopped
- 5 garlic cloves, minced
- ¼ cup ginger, grated
- 8 hot cherry peppers, diced

- 6 strips of apple wood smoked bacon
- 2 teaspoons of fresh thyme
- 3 fresh bay leaves
- 1 teaspoon black peppercorns
- 1 teaspoon wild coriander seeds
- 2 cups red wine
- ¾ cups pure maple syrup
- ½ gallon veal or chicken stock (enough to cover)
- 1 cup flour
- Paprika
- Garlic powder
- Salt & pepper

Directions:

At least 1 hour before cooking, hand rub short ribs with paprika, garlic powder, salt and pepper. Set aside at room temperature.

When you are ready to prepare, dust short ribs with light coating of flour.

Pre-heat oven to 250 degrees.

Sauté bacon in skillet over high heat until all of the grease is extracted from the bacon. Remove bacon and store. Use the hot bacon grease to braise beef for about 4 minutes on each side. Remove Ribs and set aside.

In the same grease, brown the onions, garlic, celery, and carrots for approximately 5 min. Then add cherry peppers, ginger, thyme, bay leaf, peppercorns, and coriander seeds. Cook for 3-5 minutes more.

Deglaze vegetable mixture with red wine and cook until wine is reduced (about 3 minutes).

Pour vegetable mix into a heavy, deep pan (Dutch oven) with a lid, spreading mix to cover bottom of the pan. Then set the short ribs on top of the vegetable mix with the bones facing up.

Drizzle maple syrup over short ribs; then add meat stock until the liquid is barely below the top of the short ribs. Place lid on the pan.

Bake in oven at 250 degrees for 4 hours, then raise the oven temperature to 300 degrees and cook for 1-2 hours more. Meat is ready when it is tender and falling off the bone.

Remove short ribs and trim if necessary. Place on an oven-ready service platter and tent with aluminum foil. Turn oven off and place platter in oven to keep short ribs warm.

Place pan with vegetable mix still in place over hot flame. Using a large spoon, skim off any excess grease; then reduce remaining liquid until slightly thickened (approximately 10-15 minutes).

Serve short ribs on plate and cover with sauce.

 MEAT TACOS

Ingredients:
* 1 1/2 lbs ground meat (for healthy version try ground turkey)
* 1/2 onion, diced
* 2 jalapeños, diced
* 1/4 cup cilantro, diced
* 3 cloves garlic, minced
* 1-2 tablespoons olive oil
* 3 tablespoons taco seasoning mix (see recipe)
* Salt & pepper
* 1/4 cup red wine
* 6-8 taco shells

- 6 oz grated Cheddar cheese
- Salsa (see recipe)

Directions:
Pre-heat over to 400 degrees.

In a pan on high flame, thoroughly cook meat until browned, stirring constantly and breaking up the meat. Scrape the meat into a bowl and set aside. Drain off any excess grease and juices from the meat back into the pan.

Add olive oil and then brown the onions. After 2-3 minutes, add the garlic and jalapeños.

When vegetables are brown, deglaze with red wine and let cook until wine reduces. Then add meat and mix together with taco seasoning mix, fresh cilantro, salt and pepper.

Cook for 10 minutes on medium heat.

Place taco shells on baking sheet and place in oven for 5-10 minutes until lightly brown.

Serve meat mix with taco shells, grated cheese, and salsa.

◌◌ MONGOLIAN BBQ RIBS ◌◌

This is a unique method of preparing ribs that involves boiling already braised ribs in a sweet and spicy sauce. The key is to cook the ribs until the sauce boils down into a thick caramelized sauce. The thicker the sauce gets, the more you need to stir the ribs to keep them from scorching. You can also finish these ribs over a hot grill to create a crispy crust.

Ingredients:
- 2 racks of pork ribs cut into individual pieces
- 1 onion, minced
- 2 garlic cloves, minced
- 1 inch ginger root, minced
- ⅓ cup soy sauce
- 2 tablespoons red chili paste
- 2 tablespoons brown sugar
- 1 ½ cups chicken stock
- 2 tablespoons sesame oil
- Paprika, garlic powder, salt & pepper

Directions:
Rub the ribs with paprika, garlic powder, salt & pepper. Let stand at room temperature for up to one hour.

In a large bowl, mix the onion, garlic, ginger, soy, chili paste, brown sugar, and chicken stock.

In pre-heated wok on high heat, add sesame oil and brown ribs thoroughly on all sides.

Poor mix over ribs and cook at high heat until mix begins to boil. Set heat to medium and cook until the sauce is completely reduced, stirring constantly (about 30 minutes). .

⟨ℰ RACK OF LAMB ℰ⟩

Ingredients:

- 2 racks of lamb, frenched and cut into racks of 3 chops each
- 1 cup of fine bread crumbs
- 2 tablespoons Dijon mustard
- 4 cloves of garlic, minced
- ¼ cup Italian parsley, minced
- 2 teaspoons fresh rosemary, minced
- 3 tablespoons olive oil
- Paprika, salt and pepper

Notes: Try using less oil and minimize the thickness of the bread crumb mixture on the lamb.

Directions:

Hand rub racks with salt, pepper, paprika, and minced garlic; let stand for 1 hour at room temperature.

Pre-heat oven to 450 degrees.

In pre-heated pan over high heat, add olive oil and let warm until it starts to smoke.

Brown racks on all sides; then set aside and let cool.

In a bowl, combine bread crumbs, parsley, and rosemary. Then add 2 tablespoons of olive oil until it creates a wet-sand consistency.

Coat racks with mustard and pack with the bread crumb mixture.

Place lamb racks on elevated cooking rack with the tips of the bone facing down. Bake for 15-20 minutes (medium rare); 25-30 min for medium well.

Remove, set on carving board, and cover with foil. Let stand for 10 minutes

Carve and serve.

ROAST BEEF WITH SPICY ITALIAN TOMATO SAUCE

Ingredients:
- Roast of beef 4-6 lbs
- 4 vine ripe tomatoes
- 2 tablespoons minced rosemary
- 2 tablespoons minced thyme
- 1 tablespoon minced lavender
- 1 ½ cups Italian parsley, minced
- 2 cloves garlic, minced
- 1 teaspoon red pepper flakes
- 1 ounce of red vinegar
- ½ cup olive oil
- Paprika
- Salt & pepper

Directions:
Rub beef with paprika, salt, and pepper; let sit at room temperature for up to 1 hour.

Pre-heat oven to 375 degrees.

In pre-heated pan on high heat, add 2 tablespoons of olive oil; then brown meat on all sides until dark crust starts to form (2-3 minutes each side).

In a large bowl, mix the rosemary, thyme, lavender, salt and pepper. Cut tomatoes in half and stamp the open face of the tomato halves in season mix.

Place roast in the center of a large roasting pan and line the tomatoes face down around the roast. Sprinkle remaining season mix on roast and tomatoes.

Place roasting pan in oven at 375 degrees for 45 minutes (medium rare) to one hour (medium).

Using a spatula, scrape out the tomatoes from the roasting pan and put into a food processor. Tent the roast with foil and let stand while finishing the sauce.

Using the food processor, mix the tomatoes with the parsley, garlic, red pepper flakes, red vinegar, salt, pepper, and the remaining olive oil. Blend until thoroughly mixed.

Pour mix into pot and cook over medium to high heat for 5 minutes, stirring constantly. Serve sauce over meat.

 Roasted Turkey

The secret to a great roasted turkey is to brine the turkey overnight. Try to use a fresh turkey and do not attempt to brine a "butterball" or pre-basted turkey since they will already be infused with salt.

Ingredients:
- 15-25 lb turkey, brined over night (see recipe)
- 6-8 cups of turkey stuffing (see recipe)
- 2 sticks butter, room temp until soft
- 2 teaspoons fresh thyme, minced
- 2 teaspoons fresh tarragon, minced

- 2 teaspoons fresh rosemary, minced
- 2 teaspoons fresh sage, minced
- 4 cups low salt chicken broth
- ¼ cup all purpose flour
- Salt & pepper

Directions:
In a pan over medium heat, mix ½ cup (one stick) butter with all minced herbs, salt & pepper.

Pre-heat oven to 300 degrees.

Clean and pat dry turkey.

Starting at the neck, slide your hand between the skin and breast meat to loosen skin; then rub 4 tablespoons herb butter over breast meat and under skin. Rub neck and body cavity with 4 tablespoons of herb butter. Rub body of turkey with remaining herb butter.

Fill turkey cavities with stuffing. Tuck wings under and sew body cavity together.

Wrap turkey tightly with heavy aluminum foil and place in pan.

Bake one hour for each 2 lbs of turkey.

Open foil and poke holes in bottom of foil under turkey to drain juices into baking pan.

Add chicken broth to the bottom of the pan and stir. Use juices and broth to baste turkey for 30-45 min until golden brown.

Remove and let turkey stand for 20 minutes before carving.

Remove ½ cup of juices and use for gravy (see recipe).

ROTISSERIE LEMON & HERB CHICKEN

Ingredients:
- 4 lb whole roaster chicken
- 1 stick butter, set at room temperature until soft
- 2 teaspoons fresh thyme, minced
- 2 teaspoons fresh tarragon, minced
- 2 teaspoons fresh rosemary, minced
- 2 teaspoons fresh sage, minced
- Salt & pepper
- 1 lemon cut in half
- 2 sprigs fresh thyme
- 2 sprigs fresh tarragon
- 2 sprigs fresh rosemary
- 2 sprigs fresh sage

Directions:

This dish is best done on a grill with a rotisserie. If you do not have a rotisserie, you can use a traditional oven at 350 degrees. Place chicken on an elevated rack and rotate every 20 minutes.

In a large bowl, mix ½ cup (one stick) butter with all minced herbs, salt & pepper.

Rinse clean and pat dry chicken; then place lemon and sprigs of herbs inside the chest cavity.

Set up bird on rotisserie skewer. Make sure the meat is firmly connected. Tie legs off and fold wings under themselves.

Rub herb butter over the body of the chicken, under the breast skin, and in the cavities. Then add salt & pepper to chicken.

Wrap chicken tightly with heavy aluminum foil.

Cook with rotisserie grill cover closed for 1 ½ hrs.

Remove rotisserie from grill and set chicken in a shallow pan. Remove foil and drain juices into pan.

Set rotisserie with exposed chicken back on the grill and let cook for 30 min until chicken is tender and brown. Use juices to periodically baste the chicken.

Remove and let chicken stand for at least 10 minutes before carving.

Remove ½ cup of juices and use for gravy (see gravy recipe).

SOUTHERN FRIED CHICKEN

Fried chicken is one of those dishes that are too often taken for granted. How difficult can it be? You flour up some chicken and throw it the fryer. But really good fried chicken is very hard to make, which is why you rarely hear anyone tell you about the restaurant that made best fried chicken they ever ate. Instead they will tell you how great their mother's fried chicken is, or talk about their aunt or grandmothers secret fried chicken recipe. That is because making great fried chicken requires the right mixture of love, patience and hard work that only comes from someone who really cares about the people they are cooking for.

My mother made a great fried chicken using a buttermilk batter. My mother-in-law Betty also makes a great fried chicken; however, she doesn't use a batter dip. Her secret is in how you flour the chicken. She also cuts the chicken into smaller pieces, which allows the chicken to cook more evenly. My recipe is a blend of the recipes from the two loving mothers in my life.

Beyond the basic recipe and ingredients, making great fried chicken depends on timing and temperature. You need to make sure you have the oil and the chicken at the right temperature before you start the frying process. I highly recommend using a good oil thermometer to verify the temperature. You also need to separate your dark and white meats and cook them separately. Dark meat takes slightly longer to cook and the white meat will lose its moisture if it is cooked to long.

Ingredients:
- 1 whole chicken, cut in pieces (cut breasts and thighs in half)
- 1 quart of buttermilk
- 3 sprigs each of fresh thyme, sage, oregano and parsley
- 1 small onion coarsely chopped
- 4 cloves of garlic, smashed
- 2 teaspoons Tabasco sauce
- 4 cups self-rising flour
- 2 tablespoons granulated onion
- 2 tablespoons garlic powder
- 2 tablespoons black pepper
- 1 tablespoon salt
- 1 teaspoon cayenne pepper
- 6 cups vegetable oil

For the chicken rub:
- 2 teaspoons granulated onion
- 1 teaspoon garlic powder
- 1 teaspoon black pepper
- 1 teaspoon salt

Directions:
Cut the chicken into pieces. If the breasts and thighs are small to medium sized, cut them in half. If they are larger you should cut them into thirds or quarters. Wash chicken thoroughly for at least 5

minutes to remove any excess fluids. Be careful to not cause cross contamination by splashing the chicken residue on your counters (I always spray my sink with a diluted bleach mixture after removing the chicken).

Lightly rub chicken with granulated onion, garlic powder, salt and pepper.

Place the chicken, chopped onions, smashed garlic cloves, and sprigs of herbs in a plastic food storage bag and pour in the buttermilk and Tabasco sauce. Shake it up and let stand at least 8 hours in refrigerator.

Remove the chicken and set aside, discarding the buttermilk and herb mix. Let stand at room temperature for no more than 30 minutes (the objective is to bring the meat close to room temperature before attempting to fry so that it cooks evenly).

In a bowl or bag, thoroughly mix the flour, granulated onion, garlic powder, black pepper, salt and cayenne pepper.

Flour each piece of chicken and let stand until the moisture starts to seep through the flour (the surface of the chicken will start to appear wet). This will take approximately 5-8 minutes.

Flour each piece of chicken again and let stand until the chicken starts to appear wet (about 5 minutes). The chicken is now ready to be fried.

Fill cast iron skillet 3-4 inches high with oil and heat on high flame at 340 degrees. It is recommended that you use an oil thermometer to maintain the grease temperature before each batch of chicken is placed in the oil.

Starting with the dark meat, place chicken in oil. Turn constantly until golden brown (about 15-18 minutes for the dark meat, 12-14 minutes for the white meat).

Remove chicken and place on paper towel to dry. Make sure you test at least one large piece for doneness before serving by cutting it open to the bone. There should be no evidence of blood or redness in the meat. Lightly dust with salt and fresh ground pepper.

SMOKED BABY BACK RIBS

This is the oldest recipe in my book. I have been making ribs since I was a child. Later in life I developed a BBQ restaurant concept that won quite a few awards and BBQ contests. There are three essential requirements for a great rib: 1) a good rub that is applied at lease one day before you cook; 2) slow cooking the ribs (preferably with a smoker); and 3) the sauce. The ribs should never "fall off the bone" when you eat them. Properly smoked and grilled, they will develop an almost pink color and will stay firmly attached to the bone. While this recipe may seem simple, cooking great ribs requires a lot of attention.

Ingredients:
- 2 racks baby back ribs, 1-½ to 2 pounds each
- 4-5 tablespoons BBQ rub (see recipe)
- 2 cups BBQ sauce (see recipe)
- 2 cups mesquite chips, soaked in water for at least 1 hour

Directions:
One day prior to cooking ribs, generously rub each rack with BBQ rub, pressing the spices into the meat. Tightly wrap racks with plastic wrap and refrigerate. Allow the ribs to stand at room temperature for 20 to 30 minutes before grilling.

Drain the mesquite chips and toss them directly onto the burning coals or into the smoker box of a gas grill, following manufacturer's instructions. Grill the ribs over indirect low heat (grill temperature should be about 300°F), until the meat is very tender and has shrunk back from the ends of the bones, approximately 1 hour.

After the ribs are done, start brushing occasionally with the sauce on both sides and grill until crispy.

Transfer the ribs to a sheet pan and tightly cover with aluminum foil. Let rest for 30 minutes. Serve warm.

SPICE RUBBED PORK TENDERLOIN

Ingredients:
- Pork tenderloin, 2-3 lbs
- 1 large onion, sliced
- 4 ounces shitake mushrooms, thinly sliced, stems reserved
- ½ tablespoons sliced fresh sage leaves
- 4 hot cherry peppers, sliced
- 1 tablespoon flour
- ½ cup dry white wine
- 2 cups chicken stock
- 1 teaspoon paprika
- ½ teaspoon black cumin seeds, finely ground
- ½ teaspoon dried pomegranate seeds, finely ground
- ½ teaspoon black peppercorns, finely ground
- 1 ½ teaspoons coriander seeds, finely ground
- 2 teaspoons star anise
- 1 teaspoon clove
- 1 teaspoon cinnamon
- ½ inch minced ginger root
- 3 tablespoons olive oil
- 2 tablespoons butter

Directions:

For the rub, mix together the coriander seeds, cumin seeds, dried pomegranate seeds, black peppercorns, star anise, cloves, and cinnamon.

Using ⅔ of rub mix, rub meat and set at room temperature for one hour.

In a pan on medium to high heat, add 2 tablespoons olive oil and 2 tablespoons butter; then add the sliced onion and cook until softened (3-5 minutes). Next add mushrooms, hot cherry peppers, sliced fresh sage leaves, ginger, remaining spice mix, and paprika. Cook an additional 3 minutes, and then add flour.

Deglaze pan with white wine. Cook until wine is reduced, then add the chicken stock. Reduce until thickened, about 15 minutes to make 1 cup of sauce. Pour sauce into bowl.

Pre-heat oven to 400 degrees.

Using the same pan at high heat, add remaining oil and brown tenderloin on all sides (2-3 minutes per side).

Place roast in a narrow baking pan and pour sauce over the top. Roast for 30 minutes.

TAMARIND GLAZED CHICKEN

Ingredients:
- 1 whole roaster chicken, split in half
- 4 oranges, squeezed with pulp
- 1 small red onion, finely diced
- 2 tablespoons olive oil
- 2 tablespoons minced ginger

- ½ cup rice wine
- ½ cup chicken broth
- 3 tablespoons tamarind sauce
- 1 teaspoon honey
- Salt & pepper

Directions:

Pre-heat over to 400 degrees. Rub chicken with kosher salt and fresh ground pepper. Pre-bake chicken for 45 minutes and remove.

In pre-heated pan, add olive oil and brown onions & ginger for 3-5 minutes. Deglaze pan with rice wine and let cook until wine reduces (about 3 minutes). Add chicken broth and freshly squeezed orange juice with pulp. Let cook down for about 25 minutes.

Add tamarind sauce, honey, fresh ground pepper and salt. Cook for an additional 5 minutes.

Baste chicken with sauce on both sides. Place on grill and cook until crisp, turning only once.

 Tandoori Chicken

Tandoori is a method of cooking that originated in the Middle East. The word "tandoori" derives from the Hindi word "tandoor", a cylindrical clay oven used in cooking and baking. The heat for a tandoor was traditionally generated by a charcoal fire or wood fire, burning within the tandoor itself. The food was placed directly on the sides of the clay oven, thus exposing the food to both live-fire, radiant heat cooking, and hot-air, convection cooking.

When I was a child, my parents would take us to an authentic Indian restaurant that cooked their Tandoori on an open fire clay oven. I have loved this dish ever since. This version pre-bakes the chicken and finishes it over a hot gas or coal grill.

Ingredients:
- Whole chicken, cut in pieces
- 2 tablespoons peanut or vegetable oil
- 1 onion, chopped
- Salt and pepper
- 5 cloves garlic, smashed
- 2 inches ginger, minced
- 1 tablespoon ground coriander
- 1 teaspoon ground cardamom
- 1 tablespoon paprika
- 1 teaspoon ground cumin
- Pinch of cayenne pepper
- Pinch of crushed red chili flakes
- 3 cups plain yogurt

Directions:
Pre-heat oven to 300 degrees. Place chicken in deep roasting pan with lid (Dutch oven).

In a large skillet, heat oil and add onions, salt and pepper. Cook until softened, then add garlic and ginger and cook for about 2 minutes more.

Mix in spices and cook for no more than a minute; then add yogurt.

Pour mix over chicken, cover, and bake for 1 ½ hours.

Pre-heat grill, remove excess sauce, and char until crisp on all sides (about 15 minutes)..

☙ Tuscan Pork Chops ❧

Ingredients:
- 6 one-two inch thick pork chops
- 2 shallots, diced
- 1 bulb fennel, sliced including ferns
- One handful Italian parsley, chopped
- 2 cloves garlic, minced
- 1 can (16 oz) diced tomatoes
- 2 tablespoons capers
- Zest of ½ lemon
- ¼ cup dry white wine
- ½ cup chicken broth
- 3 tablespoons olive oil
- Paprika, salt and pepper

Directions:
Rub pork with paprika, salt and pepper. Let stand at room temperature for one hour.

In a preheated pan on high heat, add 2 tablespoons olive oil and braise chops for 3-5 minutes on each side. Then remove chops and set aside.

Add remaining olive oil to pan; then add the shallots, garlic, and fennel. Cook for 3-4 minutes until vegetables begin to soften. Add 1 teaspoon salt. Reduce heat to medium.

Add one handful chopped parsley, then deglaze pan with wine. Cook until wine is reduced (approximately 3 minutes).

Stir in can of diced tomatoes, chicken broth, capers, and lemon zest.

Place chops back in pan. Cover and cook for 10 minutes, turning chops at least once.

Remove lid and cook until juices reduce (about 6-8 minutes). Sprinkle with 2 tablespoons of parsley and serve.

VEAL LEMON

Ingredients:
- 6 pieces Veal Scaloppini, pounded thin
- ½ cup sifting flour
- 2 teaspoons lemon zest
- Juice of one lemon
- 1 tablespoon Italian parsley, chopped
- 2 tablespoons capers
- 3 cloves garlic, thinly sliced
- ¼ cup dry white wine
- ½ cup chicken broth
- Paprika, salt and pepper
- ¼ cup olive oil

Directions:
Hand rub veal with paprika, salt and pepper. Set aside for at least one hour at room temp. Also remember to zest the lemon and set aside.

Just prior to cooking, lightly dust veal with sifted flour on all sides.

Pre-heat a large pan at high heat. Add olive oil and let warm for 2-3 minutes; then add sliced garlic and sear until light golden brown (about 3 minutes). Stir in the lemon zest and cook for 2-3 minutes. Strain the oil into a bowl and reserve the cooked garlic and lemon zest for later.

Put 2 tablespoons of the lemon and garlic infused oil in the pan. Add veal and brown for 2 minutes on each side. Remove the veal and set aside. If necessary, you can prepare the veal in batches and add more oil with each batch.

With the pan still hot, add the white wine, capers, lemon juice, chicken broth, and the reserved cooked garlic and lemon zest. Scrape the bottom of the pan and allow sauce to come to a boil.

Reduce heat to low and place the meat in the sauce. The sauce should just barely cover the meat. If necessary, add more chicken broth.

Cook until sauce thickens (no more than 5-7 minutes) and serve with parsley garnish.

 VEAL OSSO BUCO IN TOMATO SAUCE

This is one of my favorite dishes. The traditional Osso Buco is done milenaise style that essentially creates a brown sauce that resembles gravy and is served over risotto. I prefer a tomato base sauce that is served over pasta. The secret to this recipe is creating a bed of caramelized red onions that separates the meat from the pan. This will let you slow cook the veal shanks without scorching them. The onions will further caramelize and season the dish. You will need a heavy pot with a lid, preferably a Dutch oven.

Ingredients:
- 6 veal shanks, 2-3 inches thick
- 1 red onion, sliced thin
- 1 carrot, diced
- 2 stalks celery, diced
- 3 cloves fresh garlic, minced

- 1 ½ cups red wine
- 10 cups chicken stock
- 4 tomatoes, diced
- 3 oz tomato paste
- 1 cup sifted flour
- 1 teaspoon crushed red pepper
- Paprika, garlic powder, salt & pepper
- 4 tablespoons olive oil
- 1 lb penne pasta

Directions:
Rub veal with salt, pepper, garlic powder, and paprika; let stand for one hour at room temperature.

Just prior to cooking, coat veal with sifted flour.

Pre-heat large pan on medium to high heat; then add 2 tablespoons olive oil. Brown onion slices on both sides and then line the bottom of a large pot with lid (Dutch oven) with the grilled onions.

In the same pan, set heat to high and brown veal on all sides (about 2-3 min per side). Then remove and set in a Dutch oven with exposed bones facing up.

Set heat to medium to high and brown garlic; then add celery and carrots. When softened, add red wine to deglaze the pan. Let wine cook down until reduced. Add crushed red pepper, salt and pepper. Scrape vegetable mixture into large pot, evenly distributing it around the shanks.

Add broth to pot until almost covering the shanks.

Let cook covered under low-medium heat for one hour.

Remove cover, add tomato paste, and diced tomatoes. Cook down for approximately 30 minutes.

Serve over penne pasta.

VEAL PARMIGANO

Most versions of this dish involve breading and braising veal scaloppini. I prefer to prepare the veal with the bone in by butterflying a veal rib chop, pounding it out real thin, and hand rubbing it with spices. I also prepare my Veal with a Milanese style, with the cheese mixed with the bread crumbs. I recommend you serve this directly over a bed of my marinara sauce with pasta on the side.

Ingredients:
- 4 veal rib chops
- 1 cup Italian bread crumbs
- ¼ cup ragiano parmesan
- ¼ chopped Italian parsley
- 2 eggs beaten with 1 teaspoon water
- ¼ cup olive oil
- Paprika, garlic powder, salt and pepper
- 4 cups of marinara sauce (see recipe)

Directions:
Starting at the end of the bone, butterfly the veal rib chops evenly down the middle. Then cover the veal with plastic wrap and pound out meat using a meat hammer.

Hand rub the veal with paprika, garlic powder, salt & pepper. Let stand for at least 30 minutes at room temperature.

Combine bread crumbs, cheese, and parsley in a large bowl. Crack eggs into another large bowl. Mix in water and whip until thoroughly mixed.

Pre-heat oven to 450 degrees.

In a pre-heated pan on high heat, add 2 tablespoons of oil. Note: as you brown the veal, make sure you add just enough oil to coat the bottom of the pan.

Dip veal in egg and cover with bread and cheese mix.

Brown veal on each side for not more that 2 minutes; then place on baking sheet.

Finish in oven for 5-10 minutes.

Serve over bed of marinara sauce.

PESCATO DI MARE
(SEAFOOD)

BLACKENED TILAPIA WITH CREOLE SAUCE

CRISPY SALMON

LOBSTER RISOTTO

SCALLOPS IN TOMATO GARLIC SAUCE

SEARED SCALLOPS AND TOMATOES

SHRIMP IN CHIPOTLE COLA SAUCE

SPICY JALAPEÑO CRAB CAKES

WASABI SEA BASS

∝ BLACKENED TILAPIA ∽ WITH CREOLE SAUCE

Tilapia is the perfect fish for blackening. It is very flavorful and holds together over high heat. You can also substitute red snapper, grouper, or other "white" fish; however they are generally much more expensive than Tilapia.

Ingredients:
* 6 tilapia filets
* 3 tablespoons blackened rub (see recipe)
* 3 cups Creole sauce (see recipe)
* 2 cups cooked white rice
* 2 tablespoons minced green onions
* Olive oil
* ¼ lb butter (1 stick)

Directions:
Using a brush, lightly coat fish filets on each side with the olive oil; dust thoroughly with the blackening rub mix. Set out at room temperature for 15 minutes, turning once.

Note: It is recommended to cook blackened fish outside because of the amount of smoke that is generated.

Heat a cast iron skillet until it's almost red hot. Drop one-half of the stick of butter into the pan. As soon as the butter starts to turn brown, immediately place the filets in the skillet and cook for 2 minutes per side. Add additional butter after turning, if needed.

You can usually cook 2 or 3 filets at a time. Add more butter and allow the butter to turn brown once more before placing the additional filets in the skillet.

Serve with rice and ladle a generous amount of Creole sauce on the rice and fish. Garnish with green onions.

∽ CRISPY SALMON ∾

This is an unusual method of cooking salmon that creates a crispy crust on the dish. The key is to use clarified butter since regular butter will burn over high heat. You should use an oil thermometer to make sure the oil is at the right temperature.

Ingredients:
- 4 filets fresh salmon, skin removed
- 3 oz clarified butter
- 2 tablespoons flat leaf parsley
- Salt and pepper

Directions:
Rub salmon with salt & pepper and sprinkle with parsley. Set at room temperature for 15 minutes, turning once.

Pre-heat pan on high heat, then add clarified butter.

When butter is hot (approximately 400 degrees), brown salmon on each side until cooked (about 2-3 min per side).

Recommend serving over risotto or tomato sauce with pasta.

꩜ LOBSTER RISOTTO ꩜

Ingredients:
- Two whole live lobsters (approximately 1 ¼ lb each)
- 2 cups Arborio rice
- 2 shallots, minced
- 2 garlic cloves, minced
- 1 tablespoon parsley, chopped
- 1 tablespoon fresh tarragon, minced
- Large pinch of saffron
- 1 quart chicken broth
- 1 cup heavy cream
- ¼ stick unsalted butter
- 2 cups white wine
- 3 tablespoons olive oil
- Salt and pepper

Directions:
Place lobsters in large pot of boiling water for 2-3 minutes (until lobsters start to change color). The idea is to blanch the lobsters without fully cooking them. Remove the lobsters and rinse with cool water.

Break off the tails and make a cut up the inside of each tail to expose the meat. Remove the meat and reserve the shell. Remove the backs from the lobster body and discard the insides reserving the shell. Crack open the claws and remove the meat and reserve the shell from the claws. Chop the lobster meat in large chunks and place in the refrigerator. Thoroughly rinse all of the pieces of the shell.

Place the clean shells in a medium pot and add the chicken broth. Bring to a boil, then reduce the heat and let simmer for 20-30 minutes.

In a preheated pan on high heat, add olive oil, then add the shallots and garlic; cook them until softened (approximately 2 to 3 minutes).

Add more olive oil, then the rice to the pan and stir constantly until the rice begins to toast. You will notice a small brown spot start to form at the center of each grain of rice.

Deglaze the pan with white wine and cook until reduced.

Use a strainer to separate the shells from the broth and reserving the broth. Discard the shells.

Turn the heat to medium and start adding the stock about ½ cup at a time, stirring occasionally. Place cover over pan between stirring.

When the rice is al dente, add the lobster, cream, and crushed saffron; let cook uncovered until the cream reduces and turns a light red/orange color (approximately 4 minutes). Stir in butter, parsley, tarragon, salt and pepper, and serve.

SCALLOPS IN TOMATO GARLIC SAUCE

Ingredients:
- 1 ½ lbs sea scallops
- 5 tablespoons olive oil
- 2 shallots, diced
- 6 cloves garlic, finely minced
- 1 cup crushed tomatoes
- ½ cup dry white wine
- 1 tablespoon chopped flat leaf parsley
- 1 tablespoon diced basil
- ¼ cup flour
- Salt & pepper

Directions:
In a pre-heated pan on medium to high heat, add 2 tablespoons olive oil. Add shallots and cook until softened (about 3 minutes). Then add garlic and cook until soft but not brown (about 2 minutes). Deglaze with wine and cook until reduced (about 3-4 minutes).

Stir in tomatoes with juice, parsley, basil, salt and pepper. Reduce heat and cook until slightly thickened (about 3-5 minutes).

Set aside and keep warm.

Salt & pepper scallops, then lightly dust with flour.

In a pre-heated pan on high heat, add olive oil and brown scallops for about 1 minute per side.

Turn heat to low and gently stir in tomato sauce to coat scallops.

Recommend serving over rice or thin pasta.

SEARED SCALLOPS & TOMATOES

Ingredients:
* 1 ½ lbs sea scallops
* 2 shallots, diced
* 4 large tomatoes, sliced
* 4 cloves garlic, minced
* 1 tablespoon chopped chives
* ½ cup dry white wine
* 4 pieces apple wood-smoked bacon with fat removed
* ¼ cup flour
* Salt & pepper
* 2 tablespoons olive oil
* ½ stick butter

Directions:

Lightly salt and pepper scallops and dust with flour.

In a pre-heated pan over high heat, melt butter. As soon as butter starts to foam, sear scallops on both sides until golden brown (about 2 minutes per side). Set aside.

Add garlic to pan and brown for 2-3 minutes. Using a brush, lightly coat tomato slices with olive oil and sear in pan for 30 seconds on each side. Remove tomatoes.

Add bacon to pan and cook until crispy (about 4-5 minutes); then add shallots and cook until soft (about 3 minutes). Deglaze pan with wine and cook until reduced (about 3 minutes).

When wine is reduced, remove from heat and whisk in 8 tablespoons cold butter until sauce is emulsified. Salt & pepper to taste.

Arrange 3 tomato slices per plate, rest one scallop on each tomato, and drizzle sauce around plate. Garnish with chopped chives.

⌒⌒ SHRIMP IN ⌒⌒
CHIPOTLE COLA SAUCE

Ingredients:

- 20-30 large shrimp, peeled and deveined
- ½ cup diced white onion
- 8 cloves garlic, minced
- 4 ripe tomatoes, chopped
- ¼ cup lime juice
- 2 cans chipotles, finely minced
- ½ cup coca cola
- ¼ cup dry white wine
- ¾ teaspoon dried oregano
- Salt & pepper
- 3 tablespoons olive oil

Directions:

In a bowl, create the chipotle cola sauce by mixing the chipotles, cola, and lime juice. Mix thoroughly.

In a pre-heated pan on medium to high heat, add a tablespoon of olive oil and sauté shrimp for 2 minutes. Remove and place shrimp in a bowl and toss in bowl with chipotle cola sauce.

With heat on high, add 2 tablespoons oil to the pan, then cook onion until slightly brown (about 2-3 minutes). Add garlic and cook an additional 2-3 minutes until softened.

Add oregano, salt and pepper, then deglaze pan with wine. Cook until wine is reduced (about 3 minutes).

Reduce heat to medium and stir in tomatoes with juice. Cook 4-5 minutes, then gently stir in the shrimp and chipotle-cola sauce. Cook until sauce is reduced (about 3-4 minutes). Recommend serving over rice or thin pasta.

Spicy Jalapeno Crab Cakes

I prefer my crab cakes with very little breading or flour. The jalapeños can be omitted if you want a less spicy version.

Ingredients:

- 2 pounds lump crabmeat
- 2 cups cornmeal
- 3 tablespoons finely sifted flour
- 4 tablespoons Dijon mustard
- 2 jalapeño peppers, diced
- 2 cloves garlic, minced
- 1 yellow (sweet) onion, minced
- ¼ cup dry white wine
- ¼ cup sour cream
- Salt & pepper
- Pinch of crushed red pepper.
- 4 tablespoons olive oil
- ½ cup of Spicy Mango Salsa (see recipe)

Directions:

In a preheated pan over medium to high heat, add 1 tablespoon of olive oil. Cook onions until softened (about 3-4 minutes), then add garlic and jalapeño peppers. Add salt, pepper, and a pinch of crushed red pepper. Cook 3 minutes more.

Deglaze with white wine. Cook until wine is partially reduced (about 3-4 minutes). Remove from heat and let cool.

In a large bowl, combine onion mixture with sour cream and mustard. Then add crabmeat and flour and stir until all of the ingredients are thoroughly mixed. Cover and refrigerate for at least one hour.

Preheat oven to 400 degrees.

Create 8 crabmeat patties about 1" thick and 3" in diameter. Roll the patties in the cornmeal, coating them on both sides and the edges.

In a preheated pan on high heat, add the remaining olive oil. When oil is hot, brown the crab cakes on each side until golden brown (about 2 minutes each side).

Transfer the pan to the oven and let finish for 5 minutes.

Serve over a thin bed of Spicy Mango Salsa.

⋐ WASABI SEA BASS ⋑

Wasabi is a spice with an extremely strong flavor. It is also known as "Japanese horseradish." Most people are familiar with wasabi paste that is used to add spice to soy sauce when serving sushi. This recipe uses a mix of wasabi flavored mustard and wasabi paste. In spite of the spicy flavor of the wasabi, this dish is not spicy at all. The sea bass absorbs and neutralizes the heat from the spice. The objective with this dish is to create a crunchy crust on the outside that sears in the juice of the fish.

Ingredients:
* 6 sea bass filets cut in squares 2 inch thick and 3 inches on each side
* 6 tablespoons wasabi mustard
* 2 cups panko
* Juice of one lemon
* 1 tablespoon wasabi paste
* Salt & pepper
* ½ stick of butter
* 3 tablespoons olive oil

Directions:

Pre-heat oven to 450 degrees.

In a large bowl, thoroughly mix wasabi mustard, lemon juice, wasabi paste, salt & pepper.

Roll filets in mix, then coat liberally with panko.

In a pre-heated pan on high heat, melt 1 tablespoon butter with 1 tablespoon oil.

Brown filets on all sides (about 1 minute on each side including the ends), then remove and place on elevated baking rack.

Finish in oven for 10 minutes & serve.

CONTORNI
(SIDE DISHES)

BRAISED BRUSSELS SPROUTS

FRENCH GREEN BEANS

ITALIAN STUFFED ONIONS

LEEKS VINAIGRETTE

POTATOES LYONNAISE

SHALLOT GRAVY

STUFFED CABBAGE LEAVES

SHRIMP STUFFED AVOCADOS

SPICY BLACK BEANS IN CITRUS SAUCE

TURKEY STUFFING

BRAISED BRUSSELS SPROUTS

Ingredients:
- 1 lb Brussels sprouts, sliced in half
- ¼ lb pancetta, diced
- 4 cloves garlic, minced
- ½ cup chicken broth
- ¼ cup white wine
- 2 tablespoons fresh thyme, minced
- Paprika, salt & pepper
- 3 tablespoons olive oil

Directions:
In a large bowl, mix the Brussels sprouts, garlic, thyme, paprika, salt and pepper. Add 2 tablespoons of olive oil and mix thoroughly. Let stand at room temperature for at least one hour.

Preheat oven to 400 degrees.

In a large preheated pan on high heat, add remaining oil and brown pancetta for 4-5 minutes.

Add Brussels sprouts to pan and brown evenly on all sides.

Deglaze with white wine and cook until reduced (about 3 minutes). Stir in chicken broth and place in oven for 25 minutes, stirring at least once.

French Green Beans

Ingredients:
- 1 ½ lbs French green beans (haricot verts), stems removed
- 1 shallot, minced
- 1 teaspoon diced lemon zest
- 1 tablespoon diced Italian parsley
- 2 tablespoons olive oil
- Salt and pepper

Directions:
Fill medium sized pot with water and bring to a boil. Add beans and cook until tender but still resistant to bite.

Remove and drain beans, then plunge into cold water (add ice as necessary). This will prevent the beans from cooking with their own heat and getting too soft.

In a pre-heated pan on medium to high heat, heat the oil then add shallots and cook until softened (about 2-3 minutes).

Add beans and sauté until brown (about 4-5 minutes). Then stir in lemon zest and cook 1 minute. Season with salt and pepper to taste.

Serve with parsley garnish.

ITALIAN STUFFED ONIONS

Ingredients:
- ½ lb thick pancetta, diced
- 6 white onions, peeled and cut in half
- 1 egg
- 3 tablespoons plain bread crumbs
- 2 oz milk
- 1 cup grated Parmesan
- 1 teaspoon kosher salt
- 1 teaspoon pepper
- ½ stick butter

Directions:
Add 1 inch of water to a large pan and bring to a boil.

Place onion halves face down in boiling water. Lower heat to medium and simmer for 5-10 minutes until core of onions begin to soften.

Take baking dish and coat bottom with butter (rub stick on dish to create thin film to prevent onions from sticking, and then slice remaining butter and place in dish).

Remove onions from water and place face up. Using a small fork, remove the inside of the onion, leaving at least 2-3 layers of shell.

In a small bowl, mix the milk and bread crumbs and let stand until it thickens. Set aside.

Preheat oven to 400 degrees.

Using a food processor, blend the insides of the onion and pour them into a large bowl. Add the Parmesan cheese, egg, pancetta, bread crumb mix, salt and fresh ground pepper. Mix thoroughly.

Fill the onion shells in the pan with the onion mix.

Bake for 45 min to 1 hour (until top is golden brown).

Remove and let stand for at least 10 minutes before serving.

LEEKS VINAIGRETTE

Ingredients:
- 8 leeks, trimmed but roots intact
- 2 tablespoons diced flat leaf parsley
- 1 ½ cups chicken stock
- 1 tablespoon lemon juice
- 1 ½ teaspoons Dijon mustard
- 3 tablespoons olive oil
- Salt & pepper

Directions:
Cut leeks in half lengthwise using root to keep them together.

In a pan large enough to fit the leeks in a single layer, heat 2 tablespoons olive oil on medium to high heat. Sauté leeks until lightly brown (about 5 minutes).

Add stock and parsley and bring to a simmer.

Cover and cook until tender; then transfer to a serving platter.

In the same pan, whisk 1 tablespoon olive oil, lemon juice, and mustard. Season with salt & pepper.

Pour over leeks and serve.

POTATOES LYONNAISE

Ingredients:
* 12 small white potatoes, peeled and sliced thin
* 2 tablespoons Italian parsley, minced
* 1 yellow onion, sliced thin
* ½ cup chicken stock
* 2 tablespoons unsalted butter
* 2 tablespoons olive oil
* Salt & pepper

Directions:
In a pre-heated pan on medium to high heat, add 1 tablespoon butter plus 1 tablespoon olive oil, then sauté onions until caramelized (about 4-5 minutes). Place onions in a bowl.

In the same pan, add ½ tablespoon of butter & oil and brown potatoes in separate batches. Add butter as necessary. Place in bowl with onions and stir together.

Return potatoes and onions to pan and add stock. Cover and boil for 2 minutes.

Uncover and cook until stock is reduced.

Remove from heat and stir in parsley, salt & pepper.

 SHALLOT GRAVY

Ingredients:
* One medium sized shallot, diced
* 2 tablespoons Italian parsley
* ½ stick butter

- ½ tablespoon flour
- 2 tablespoons cream
- ¼ cup white wine
- 1 cup chicken broth
- Juice reserved from meat fat
- Salt and pepper

Directions:
In a pre-heated pan on medium to high heat, add butter. When butter foams, add the shallots and cook until slightly brown (about 4-5 minutes).

Whisk in flour and then add salt & pepper. Let cook 3-4 min.

Stir in wine, chicken broth, and a touch of cream. Let cook down for approximately 5 minutes.

Stir in parsley about 3 minutes before serving.

 STUFFED CABBAGE LEAVES

Ingredients:
- 1 head Savoy cabbage
- 2 garlic cloves, minced
- 8 oz leeks, minced
- 4 oz cremini mushrooms, minced (can substitute with shitake)
- 2-3 tablespoons lemon juice
- 1 egg, beaten
- 1 cup chicken broth
- 2 teaspoons paprika
- 2 tablespoons unsalted butter
- Salt and pepper
- White wine

Directions:
In a large pot, blanch leaves in boiling salt water or steam, then cut away stems. Remove as whole cabbage leaves to create 6-8 shells. Set aside.

Use remaining cabbage to create 2 cups of minced cabbage.

Melt butter in pan, add garlic, leeks, mushrooms, then minced cabbage. Stir frequently for 10 minutes. Deglaze with white wine and let cook down for 3-5 minutes.

Stir in lemon juice and paprika. Cook for 5 minutes.

Remove from heat, pour into a bowl, and let cool.

Mix in beaten egg, salt & pepper.

Roll the stuffing mix in the leaves and place joint-side down in a baking dish. Pour broth around them and bake for 20 minutes.

 SHRIMP STUFFED AVOCADO'S

Ingredients:
- 3 whole avocados
- 1 lb cooked baby shrimp, peeled and deveined
- 2 tablespoons fat free or light mayonnaise
- 1 tablespoon lemon juice
- 1 tablespoon extra virgin olive oil
- 1 tablespoon Italian parsley, minced
- Salt and pepper

Directions:
In a large bowl, thoroughly mix the shrimp, mayo, lemon juice, and

olive oil. Cover and place in the refrigerator for at least one hour until fully chilled.

Add parsley, salt and pepper to shrimp mix.

Cut the avocados in half, leaving the shell intact and removing the seed. Remove just enough avocados from the center to create a "bowl."

Scoop the shrimp mix into the avocado bowls. Dish can be covered and refrigerated for up to one hour before serving.

SPICY BLACK BEANS IN CITRUS SAUCE

Ingredients:
- 1 lb black beans, washed
- 1 yellow (sweet) onion, diced
- 3 garlic cloves, minced
- 1 ancho chile pepper, diced
- 1 red bell pepper, diced
- 2 tablespoons cilantro, minced
- Zest and juice of one orange
- Zest and juice of ½ lemon
- 2 cups chicken broth
- ½ cup dry white wine
- 2 bay leaves
- 1 tablespoon dried Mexican oregano
- ½ teaspoon cumin
- 1 ½ teaspoons crushed red pepper
- 3 tablespoons olive oil
- Salt & pepper

Directions:

Place beans in a pot and add chicken broth. Add enough water so that the liquid is 3 times the height of the beans. Add bay leaves and oregano and bring to boil over high heat.

Skim surface for foam and reduce heat to low. Cover and cook at least 1 hour until the beans are tender. Then drain the beans while reserving at least ½ of the broth for later use. Discard bay leaves.

Pre-heat large pot on high heat and add the olive oil. Sauté onion and garlic until soft (about 3-4 minutes). Then add diced chile, bell pepper, and cilantro. Cook until vegetables are tender (about 3-4 minutes).

Stir in orange and lemon zests, cumin, crushed red pepper, salt & pepper. Deglaze pan with wine and cook until reduced (about 3 minutes).

Add beans and 2 cups of the reserved broth. Reduce heat and simmer for 15-20 minutes. Add more broth as necessary to keep beans moist.

Stir in orange and lemon juice. Add salt and pepper to taste.

ᴄ℞℮ Tᴜʀᴋᴇʏ Sᴛᴜғғɪɴɢ ℘℞⊃

This recipe has been handed down for at least 3 generations of my family. The original recipe uses 2 cans of frozen oysters and chicken giblets that would be cooked with the chicken broth. Over the years I have taken these ingredients out to make a fresher version.

Ingredients:
*   1 whole roasting chicken, cut in quarters
*   15 large stalks of celery, chopped

- 3 white onions, chopped
- 3 bell peppers, chopped
- 6 green onions, chopped
- 2 bunches regular parsley, chopped
- 8 cloves garlic, minced
- 3 large baking pans of corn bread
- 8 cups chicken broth
- 3 oz chicken bullion
- ¼ cup fresh sage, minced
- ¼ cup fresh thyme, minced
- 2 tablespoons fresh oregano, minced
- 1 cup white wine
- Salt & pepper

Directions:
Prepare cornbread per the instructions on the box and set aside to cool.

Place chicken in a large pot with a mixture of half water and ½ chicken broth. Add chicken bullion to taste. Bring to a boil, then reduce to simmer.

In a large bowl, mix together all of the vegetables and spices.

Transfer ½ of vegetable mix to the pot with chicken. Let cook covered for at least 2 hours.

Strain vegetables and chicken from the pot, reserving the liquid for use later. Let chicken and vegetables cool to touch before the next step.

Preheat oven to 350 degrees.

Remove bones from chicken/vegetable mix and then mix with fresh vegetable mix.

Add corn bread and wine to vegetable mix. Mix stuffing, using chicken broth to create a thick yet sticky consistency.

Place in a deep baking dish and bake for 1 hour.

SALSE E CONDIMENTI
(SAUCES AND SEASONINGS)

BBQ RUB

BLACKENED RUB

CREOLE SAUCE

CREOLE SEASONING MIX

FRESH KETCHUP

GINGER-SOY DIPPING SAUCE

JALAPEÑO BALSAMIC WINE REDUCTION

JAMAICAN JERK MARINADE

MARK'S CAJUN BBQ SAUCE

PORT WINE REDUCTION

SPICY MANGO SALSA

SPICY MARINADE

TACO SEASONING

TURKEY BRINE

 **BBQ R**UB

This rub will really enhance any grilled meats or chicken. You can make this rub in advance and store at room temperature. I prefer to apply the rub the day before cooking, wrap the meat tightly in plastic wrap, and refrigerate. This allows the rub to fully permeate the meat.

Ingredients:
- ½ cup fine brown sugar
- 2 tablespoons salt
- 2 tablespoons celery seeds
- 2 tablespoons garlic powder
- 2 tablespoons paprika
- 3 teaspoons ancho chile powder
- 5 teaspoons black pepper
- 5 teaspoons white pepper
- 2 teaspoons cayenne pepper
- 1 teaspoon ground clove
- ½ teaspoon ground cumin
- ½ teaspoon dried marjoram
- ½ teaspoon ground nutmeg
- ½ teaspoon dry mustard powder
- ½ teaspoon ground coriander

Directions:
In a large bowl, thoroughly mix all ingredients. Store for later use.

BLACKENED **R**UB

This is a great rub for seafood and chicken. Make sure you apply the rub at least one hour prior to cooking, to allow the rub to infuse its flavor into the dish. You can make multiple servings of this rub and store at room temperature for later use.

Ingredients:
- 1 tablespoon paprika
- 2 teaspoons onion powder
- 2 teaspoons garlic powder
- 1 teaspoon dried oregano
- 1 teaspoon dried thyme
- 2 teaspoons cayenne pepper
- 1 teaspoon white pepper
- 2 teaspoons salt
- 1 teaspoon black pepper

Directions:
Place all ingredients in a plastic storage bag, close, and shake until thoroughly mixed.

This mix can be stored indefinitely and used later.

CREOLE SAUCE

Ingredients:
- 1 medium onion, chopped
- 1 green bell pepper, chopped
- 2 celery ribs, chopped
- 5 garlic cloves, diced
- 3 shallots, chopped
- 2 teaspoons Creole seasoning mix (see recipe)
- 1 teaspoon hot paprika
- ⅛ teaspoon cayenne pepper
- 4 imported bay leaves
- 1 ¼ cups chicken stock or canned broth
- 4 medium tomatoes, peeled, seeded, and diced
- 1 tablespoon Worcestershire sauce

- 1 teaspoon hot sauce
- 2 tablespoons unsalted butter
- ½ teaspoon salt

Directions:
In a large pan or cast iron skillet on medium to high heat, melt butter, then add the onions, bell pepper, and celery. Sauté until vegetables are softened (about 3-5 minutes). Add garlic and shallots and cook for an additional 3 minutes.

Add the Creole seafood seasoning, paprika, cayenne pepper, bay leaves, and chicken stock. Bring to a boil and cook until slightly reduced and thickened, about 5 minutes.

Stir in the tomatoes and cook for 10 minutes longer until thick. Stir in the Worcestershire sauce, hot sauce, salt, and reduce the heat to low. Simmer for 10 minutes.

Serve over rice with seafood.

CREOLE SEASONING MIX

Ingredients:
- 2 tablespoons onion powder
- 2 tablespoons garlic powder
- 2 tablespoons dried oregano leaves
- 2 tablespoons dried sweet basil
- 1 tablespoon dried thyme leaves
- 1 tablespoon black pepper
- 1 tablespoon white pepper
- 1 tablespoon cayenne pepper
- 1 tablespoon celery seed
- 5 tablespoons sweet paprika

Directions:

In a large bowl, thoroughly mix all ingredients. Store for later use.

FRESH KETCHUP

After visiting a restaurant that served fresh ketchup, I was determined to create my own. Homemade ketchup is much better than any store-bought ketchup. I use fennel and cumin in my version, but you can also use garlic or hot peppers to create different flavored ketchups.

Ingredients:
- ½ yellow (sweet) onion, diced
- 1 stalk of fennel, diced
- 6 tomatoes, diced
- 1 14 oz can tomato sauce
- 1 tablespoon tomato paste
- 2 teaspoons cumin
- ½ cup brown sugar
- ½ cup cider vinegar
- 1 teaspoon oregano
- 2 tablespoons olive oil
- ½ teaspoon salt

Directions:

In a 4-quart heavy saucepan over medium to high heat, add olive oil. Sauté onion and fennel until softened (about 5 minutes).

Add tomatoes, tomato sauce, tomato paste, brown sugar, vinegar, oregano, cumin and salt. Bring to a boil, and then reduce heat to simmer and cook covered for at least 1 hour, stirring occasionally. Make sure you stir more frequently toward the end of cooking, to prevent scorching.

Using hand blender, purée the ketchup until smooth. Note: Use caution when blending hot liquids. Cook uncovered on simmer for at least 30 minutes until sauce thickens. You can add more brown sugar to achieve desired taste.

Cover and chill in refrigerator for at least 2 hours.

 GINGER-SOY DIPPING SAUCE

This is a good sauce for wontons, summer rolls and sushi dishes.

Ingredients:
- 4 tablespoons rice wine
- ⅓ cup light soy
- 1 ½ tablespoons brown sugar
- 1 tablespoon sesame oil
- 1 tablespoon sriracha sauce
- 1 tablespoon finely minced ginger
- 2 teaspoons red chile sauce

Directions:
In small food processor, thoroughly mix all ingredients.

 JALAPENO BALSAMIC WINE REDUCTION

This is a great sauce for use with red meats. It is not really spicy since the heat from the jalapenos is balanced by the sugar in the wine, vinegar and jam. I like to use this sauce over a grilled steak.

Ingredients:
- ¼ stick butter

- 2 fresh jalapeños, sliced thin
- 1/8 cup balsamic vinegar
- ¼ cup port wine
- 2 tablespoons berry jam

Directions:
In a pre-heated pan on medium to high heat, melt butter.

As soon as the butter foams, add the jalapeños and cook on both sides until lightly browned (about 3-4 minutes).

Stir in balsamic vinegar, port wine, and jam and cook until reduced (about 5-8 minutes).

Reduce to simmer until ready to serve.

JAMAICAN JERK MARINADE

This is the perfect marinade for grilled chicken and steaks. If you cannot find Scotch Bonnet peppers, you can substitute with their South American cousin - the Habanero pepper. Scotch Bonnets and Habaneros are some of the hottest of all peppers, so you may want to start with a little and add more to achieve your desired flavor. I prefer to marinate meat overnight in a sealed plastic bag.

Ingredients:
- 5 cloves garlic
- ½ cup red onions
- 3 tablespoons Jamaican Thyme
- 2 tablespoons brown sugar
- ¼ cup green onions
- 3 tablespoons ginger
- 1 teaspoon clove
- 2 teaspoons cinnamon

- 1 teaspoon allspice
- 3 tablespoons olive oil
- Salt & pepper
- 2 diced scotch bonnet peppers
- ½ cup orange juice
- 2 tablespoons lemon juice

Directions:
Thoroughly mix all ingredients in a large food processor.

Note: When using to marinade red meat, I like to serve the meat with a garlic and lemon paste as a garnish. Create the paste by mixing minced cilantro, minced green onion, minced garlic, and lemon paste (use the pulp and juice of 1 lemon to 1 clove garlic and 1 tablespoon cilantro). Mix in a little Habanero pepper for a nice kick.

Marks Cajun BBQ Sauce

This is the sauce that we used to win the annual Ribfest in Gatlinburg, Tennessee. The secret to this sauce is burning ½ of the onions, and I do mean burn them to a crisp until the onions turn into charcoal. When added to the sauce, the burnt onions introduce a nice smoky flavor and an interesting crunch to the bite.

Ingredients:
- 1 white onion, diced and separated into two even piles
- 3 cloves garlic, sliced
- 32 oz of tomato ketchup (see recipe)
- ½ cup brown molasses
- ½ cup red wine
- 3 tablespoons olive oil
- ¼ cup yellow mustard
- 3 teaspoons Tabasco sauce

- 3 tablespoons lemon juice
- 2 tablespoons Worcestershire sauce
- 1 teaspoon crushed red pepper
- Cayenne pepper
- Salt & pepper

Directions:
In a large sauce pan, heat tomato ketchup with molasses, Tabasco, cayenne pepper, mustard, salt, pepper, and lemon juice.

Pre-heat pan on medium to high heat and add 2 tablespoons olive oil. Brown ½ of the onions (about 3-5 minutes), then add garlic and crushed red pepper. Then deglaze with wine and cook until reduced (about 3 minutes). Add to sauce.

In the same pan, turn heat to high and add remaining olive oil. Add remaining onion and cook until blackened (it must be as black and hard as charcoal). Add to the sauce.

Cook until thickened and let simmer for at least 1 hour.

 PORT WINE REDUCTION

Ingredients:
- ¼ stick butter
- 1/8 cup balsamic vinegar
- ¼ cup port wine
- 2 tablespoons berry jam

Directions:
In a pre-heated pan on medium to high heat, melt butter.

As soon as the butter foams, stir in balsamic vinegar, port wine, and jam and cook until reduced (about 5-8 minutes).

Reduce to simmer until ready to serve..

 Spicy Mango Salsa

Ingredients:
- 2 mangos, mashed
- 2 tablespoon chili paste
- 2 tablespoon lime juice
- 2 teaspoon honey
- Salt & pepper

Directions:
Mix all ingredients in a bowl. Use hand blender to finely mix.

Refrigerate for at least one hour before serving.

 Spicy Marinade

Ingredients:
- ½ cup Tabasco sauce
- Juice of two lemons
- 2 cloves garlic
- ¼ cup cider vinegar
- ¼ cup warm water
- 2 tablespoons brown sugar
- 1 teaspoon salt
- 1 teaspoon pepper

Directions:
In small food processor, thoroughly mix all ingredients.

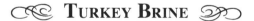 TACO SEASONING

Taco seasoning is easy to make and is much healthier than the prepackaged product in stores. I make large batches and store at room temperature for later use.

Ingredients:
- 2 tablespoons chili powder
- 2 teaspoons cumin
- 2 teaspoons oregano
- 2 teaspoons paprika
- 1 teaspoon crushed red chili peppers

Directions:
Place all ingredients in a plastic storage bag, close, and shake until thoroughly mixed.

This mix can be stored indefinitely and used later.

TURKEY BRINE

The secret to a great roasted turkey is to brine the turkey overnight. Try to use a fresh turkey and do not attempt to brine a "butterball" or pre-basted turkey, since they will already be infused with salt.

Ingredients:
- 1 fresh whole turkey
- 7 quarts (24 ounces) water
- 1 ½ cups coarse salt
- 6 bay leaves
- 2 tablespoons whole coriander seeds
- 1 tablespoon dried juniper berries
- 2 tablespoons whole black peppercorns

- 1 tablespoon fennel seeds
- 1 teaspoon black or brown mustard seeds
- 1 bottle dry Riesling wine
- 2 medium onions, thinly sliced
- 6 crushed garlic cloves
- 1 bunch fresh thyme
- Large brining bag (can substitute with a heavy duty garbage bag)

Directions:
In a large pot, bring 1 quart water, salt, bay leaves, and spices to a simmer, stirring until salt has dissolved. Let mixture cool for 5 minutes.

Line a 5-gallon container or cooler with a large brining bag. Place turkey in bag. Add salt mixture, remaining 6 quarts (24 cups) water, and the other ingredients. Tie bag. Refrigerate for 24 hours, flipping turkey once during this period.

Ancho Chile Peppers: This is the dried version of the Poblano chile and is the most common dried pepper in Mexico. This is a mild to medium-hot pepper that averages 4" long with a very dark brown color. The ancho pepper is sweeter than the ripe chile. Scoville Heat Units 2,500 - 3,000.

Andouille Smoked Sausage: Andouille (pronounced "ahn-DOO-wee") is a Cajun smoked sausage made from pork butt, shank and a small amount of pork fat, and is seasoned with salt, cracked black pepper, and garlic. True andouille is stuffed into the beef middle casing which makes the sausage approximately one and a half inches in diameter. When smoked, it becomes very dark to almost black in color. It is not uncommon for Cajun chefs to smoke andouille for seven to eight hours at approximately 175 degrees. Andouille sausages are sometimes referred to as Hot Link sausages.

Balsamic Vinegar: Although balsamic vinegar is considered wine vinegar, it is not wine vinegar at all. True balsamic vinegar is a condiment originating from Italy that is made from a reduction of syrup from sweet wine grape pressings that have never been permitted to ferment into wine. There are three types of Balsamic vinegar:

1. Traditional balsamic vinegar, which will include the official label *Balsamico Tradizionale*, originates from the Modena and Reggio Emilia areas of Italy and is aged for a minimum of 12 years. It is very expensive (can cost over $100 per bottle) and is most often served in drops on top of chunks of Parmigiano Reggiano as an antipasto.

2. Commercial grade Balsamic vinegars, such as *Balsamic Vinegar of Modena*, are mass produced to imitate the traditional product. They are made of wine vinegar with the addition of coloring, caramel, and sometimes thickeners like corn starch. There is no aging involved. Commercial grade balsamic vinegar

should be used in salad dressings, marinades, reductions, and sauces. They are the least expensive and typically found on your grocers' shelves.

3. Condimento grade products are often a mix of the two above. Condimento balsamic vinegars may be labeled as *condimento balsamico, salsa balsamica* or *salsa di mosto cotto*. Condimento balsamic vinegar may be made in the traditional way but without proper aging or from approved regions. It is typically used as a less expensive substitute for traditional balsamic vinegar.

Chinese Black Mushrooms: These dried mushrooms are often called "flower mushrooms." They can be found in Asian grocery stores and range in price from moderate to quite expensive. The name is a bit of a misnomer, since Chinese black mushrooms can be light brown, dark brown, and even gray. When it comes to cooking, it is better to use dried mushrooms, as the drying process gives them a stronger flavor.

Chipotle Chilies: Chipotle chilies are smoked jalapeño chilies that are canned in a red sauce of tomato puree, paprika, salt, onions, oil, vinegar, garlic, bay leaves, and oregano.

Clarified Butter: Clarified butter is produced by melting butter and allowing the different components to separate by density. Clarified butter has a higher smoke point than regular butter, and is therefore preferred in some cooking applications, such as sautéing. Clarified butter also has a much longer shelf life than fresh butter. To make clarified butter, melt unsalted butter and remove the foam that rises to the top with a spoon.

Gruyère Cheese: Gruyere cheese is a hard yellow cheese made from cow's milk, named after the town of Gruyères in Switzerland. There exists a French Gruyère-style cheese which must have holes similar to Swiss cheese, according to French agricultural law. Gruyère is sweet and slightly salty, with a flavor that varies widely with age.

Leeks: Leeks look like over-sized green onions. Rather than forming a tight bulb like the onion, the leek produces a long cylinder of bundled leaf sheaths. The edible portions of the leek are the white onion base and light green stalk. Leek has a mild onion-like taste, although less bitter. The taste might be described as a mix of mild onion and cucumber. It has a fresh smell, similar to onion.

Lemon Zest: Lemon zest is made from the grated peel of the lemon. It provides an intense lemon flavor and is typically used in sauces. An easy method to produce lemon zest is to shave the peel with a potato peeler and mince it thoroughly in a miniature food processor.

Mascarpone Cheese: Mascarpone cheese is a triple-cream cheese made from *crème fraîche*. Mascarpone is milky-white in color, spreads easily, and smells like milk and sweet cream. It is the main ingredient of tiramisu and is sometimes used instead of butter or Parmesan cheese, to thicken and enrich risotto.

Pancetta: Italian pancetta is a type of dry cured meat made from pork belly that has been salt cured and spiced. It is also known as Italian bacon.

Panko: Panko is a Japanese breadcrumb used to create a crunchy coating for fried foods. Panko is made from bread without crusts, resulting in a crisper, airier texture than most types of other breading.

Parmesan Cheese: This is hard, sharp, and dry Italian cheese made from skim cow's milk. This cheese is typically aged: 12-16 months. It is made all over the world, but the best quality is Italy's Parmigiano-Reggiano, which is often aged 2 years or more.

Pecorino Cheese: Pecorino is the name of a family of hard Italian cheeses made from sheep's milk. The word *pecora*, from which the name derives, means sheep. Most are aged and sharp. Pecorino Romano is most often used in pasta dishes. It has a distinctive, strong, and very salty flavor.

Saffron: Saffron is a spice that originates from the flower of the saffron crocus. Saffron tastes almost like hay and is slightly bitter. Saffron provides a yellow-orange coloring to foods and is widely used in Middle-Eastern and Asian cuisines.

Scotch Bonnet Pepper: The Scotch Bonnet is a chili pepper that comes from the same family as the habanero pepper. It is found mainly in the Caribbean islands and Jamaica. It has a distinct, almost smoky flavor that gives Jerk dishes their unique flavor. Just like the habanero, it is one of the hottest peppers in the world. Most Scotch Bonnets have a heat rating of 100,000–350,000 Scoville Units. For comparison, most jalapeños have a heat rating of 2,500 to 8,000 on the Scoville scale.

Serrano Chiles: The Serrano Chile is similar in shape but smaller and hotter than a Jalapeño. The flavor is much more intense than the jalapeño and is commonly used in spicy salsas. They are about five times hotter than jalapeños, with a heat rating of 7,000 - 25,000 on the Scoville scale.

Shallots: The shallot is in the onion family, and tastes like an onion with a sweeter, milder flavor. Shallots look more like garlic in that they are formed in a head consisting of multiple cloves. Shallots have a firm texture and provide a sweet, aromatic flavor.
Shallots are sometimes confused with scallions (also known as green onions) because in some countries, green onions are called shallots.

Sriracha Sauce: *Sriracha* sauce is the generic name for the Thai-style hot sauce named after the seaside city of Si Racha, Thailand, where it was first produced for the local seafood restaurants. This sauce is made from chili peppers, vinegar, garlic, sugar and salt. *Sriracha* sauce is a common condiment in most Asian restaurants around the world.

Tamarind Sauce: Tamarind sauce is a sweet-and-sour sauce common to Central Thailand that is made from the fruit pulp of the Tamarind tree. When harvested early, the hard green pulp of the fruit is very sour and acidic and is often used in spicy dishes. When fully ripened the Tamarind fruit is somewhat sweeter and is used in desserts and sweetened drinks.

Wasabi: Wasabi is known as "Japanese horseradish" and is a member of the family of vegetables that include horseradish and mustard. Its flavor is more like hot mustard than a chili pepper, producing vapors that stimulate the nasal passages more than the tongue. Wasabi is traditionally used as a seasoning for sushi and seafood dishes.

Listed below are some of the organizations that provide help to individuals and families. This is not intended to be an endorsement of any organization or its mission. I just wanted you to know that there are a lot of people and organizations out there who truly do want to help.

Organization	Address	Phone	Website	
AARP	601 E Street, NW Washington, DC 20049	(888) 687-2277	www.aarp.org	A nonprofit, nonpartisan membership organization that helps people 50 and over improve the quality of their lives.
Al-Anon and Alateen	1600 Corporate Landing Pkwy. Virginia Beach, VA 23454	(888) 4AL-ANON/ (888) 425-2666	www.al-anon.org	Al-Anon Family Groups are a fellowship of relatives and friends of alcoholics who share their experience, strength and hope in order to solve their common problems.
Alcoholics Anonymous	475 Riverside Dr. New York, NY 10115	(212) 870-3400	www.aa.org	A fellowship of men and women who share their experience, strength and hope with each other that they may sole their common problem and help others to recover from alcoholism.
Alzheimer's Association	225 N. Michigan Ave. Chicago, IL 60601	(800) 272-3900	www.alz.org	The leading voluntary health organization in Alzheimer care, support and research.
Alzheimer's Disease Education & Referral Center	PO Box 8250 Silver Spring, MD 20907	(800) 438-4380	www.nia.nih.gov/ alzheimers	Web site provides current, comprehensive Alzheimer's disease information and resources from the National Institute on Aging.
America Cancer Society	PO Box 22718 Oklahoma City, OK 72123	(800)ACS-2345	www.cancer.org	The organization dedicated to eliminating cancer as a major health problem by preventing cancer, saving lives and diminishing suffering from cancer through research, education, advocacy and service.

America Association for Geriatric Psychiatry	7910 Woodmont Ave Bethesda, MD 20814	(301) 654-7850	www.aagpgpa.org	AAGP is dedicated to promoting the mental health and well being of older people and improving the care of those with late-life mental disorders.
American Association of Homes and Services for the Aging	2519 Connecticut Ave., NW Washington, D.C. 20008	(202) 783-2242	www.aahsa.org	The members of the AAHSA help millions of individuals and their families every day through mission-driven, not-for-profit organizations dedicated to providing the services that people need, when they need them, in the place they call home.
American Bar Association	321 N. Clark St. Chicago, IL 60654	(800) 285-2221	www.findlegal-help.org	This site will guide consumers to a list of legal resources in their state.
American Diabetes Association	1701 North Beauregard St. Alexandria, VA 22311	(800) DIABE-TES	www.diabetes.org	Works towards the mission of preventing and curing diabetes and to improving the lives of all people affected by diabetes.
American Heart Association	7272 Greenville Ave. Dallas, TX 75231	(800) 242-8721	www.american-heart.org	Actively works to build healthier lives, free of cardiovascular diseases and stroke.
American Psychological Association	750 First St. NE Washington, D.C. 20002	(800) 374-2721	www.apa.org	Advances the creation, communication and application of psychological knowledge to benefit society and improve people's lives.
American Society on Aging	833 Market St. Suite 511 San Francisco, CA 94103	(800) 537-9728	www.asaging.org	An organization of multidisciplinary professionals in the field of aging whose resources, publications and educational opportunities are geared to enhance the knowledge and skills of people working with older adults and their families.

American Stroke Association	7272 Greenville Ave. Dallas, TX 75231	(800) 242-8721	www.strokeassociation.org	The American Stroke Association focuses on reducing risk, disability and death from stroke through research, education, fund raising and advocacy.
Americans for Better Care of the Dying	1700 Diagonal Rd. Suite 635 Alexandria, VA 22314	(703) 647-8505	www.abcd-caring.org	Aims to improve end-of-life care by learning which socials and political changes will lead to enduring, efficient and effective programs.
Arthritis Foundation	PO Box 7669 Atlanta, GA 30357	(800) 283-7800	www.arthritis.org	Helps people take control of arthritis by providing public health education; pursuing legislation; and conducting evidence based programs to improve the quality of life for people living with arthritis.
Centers for disease control	1600 Clifton Rd. Atlanta, GA 30333	(800) CDC-INFO/ (800) 232-4636	www.cdc.gov	The CDC collaborates to create the expertise, information and tools that people and communities need to protect their health - through health promotion, prevention of disease, injury and disability, and preparedness for new health threats.
Donate Life America	700 N. Fourth St. Richmond, VA 23219	(804) 782-4920	www.donatelife.net	Strives to educate and inspire people to save and enhance lives through eye tissue and organ donation.
Elder Care Locator		(800) 677-1116	www.eldercare.gov	The first step for finding local agencies in every U.S. community that can help older persons and their families access home and community-based services like transportation, meals, home care and caregiver support services.
Emotions Anonymous	PO Box 4245 Paul, MN 55104	(651) 647-9712	www.emotionsanonymous.org	A twelve-step organization composed of people who come together in weekly meetings for the purpose of working toward recovery from emotional difficulties.

Feeding America	35 E Wacker Dr. Suite 2000 Chicago, IL 60601	(800) 771-2303	www.feedingamerica.org	Feeding America provides food assistance to low-income people facing hunger in the United States through a network of food banks, soup kitchens, school programs and emergency shelters.
Gamblers Anonymous	PO Box 17173 Los Angeles, CA 90017	(213) 386-8789	www.gamblersanonymous.org	A fellowship of men and women who share the experience, strength and hope with each other that they may solve their problem and help others to recover from a gambling problem.
Homeownership Preservation Foundation	3033 Excelsior Blvd., Suite 500 Minneapolis, MN 55416	(888) 955-HOPE	www.995hope.org	The Homeownership Preservation Foundation can provide answers, connection to a counselor, and comprehensive telephone counseling to help homeowners avoid foreclosure.
Hospice Foundation of America	1621 Connecticut Ave., NW Washington, D.C. 20009	(800) 854-3402	www.hospicefoundation.org	Exists to help those who cope both personally or professionally with terminal illness, death, and the process of grief and bereavement.
Law Help	151 West 30th St. New York, NY 10001	(212) 760-2554	www.lawhelp.org	Helps low and moderate income people find free aid programs in their communities, and answers to questions about their legal rights.
Legal Services Corporation	3333 K Street, NW Washington, DC 20007	(202) 295-1500	www.lsc.gov	Promotes equal access to justice and provides high quality civil legal assistance to low-income persons.
Marijuana Anonymous	PO Box 2912 Van Nuys, CA 91404	(800) 766-6779	www.marijuana-anonymous.org	A fellowship of men and women who share the experience, strength and hope with each other that they may solve their problem and help others to recover from marijuana addiction.

Mental Health America	2000 N. Beauregard St. Alexandria, VA 22311	(800) 969-6642	www.mental-healthamerica.net	The goal of Mental Health America is to educate the general public about the realities of mental health and mental illness.
Mental Health Services Locator	PO Box 2345 Rockville, MD 20847	(800) 789-2647	www.mental-health.org	Provides information about mental health for users of mental health services and their families, the general public, policy makers, providers, and the media.
Narcotics Anonymous	PO Box 9999 Van Nuys, CA 91409	(818) 773-9999	www.na.org	A nonprofit fellowship of men and women for whom drugs had become a major problem.
National Alliance on Mental Health	2107 Wilson Blvd., Suite 300 Arlington, VA 22201	(800) 950-NAMI /(800) 950-6264	www.nami.org	A grassroots mental health organization dedicated to improving the lives of individuals and families affected by mental illness.
National Campaign to Prevent Teen and Unplanned Pregnancy	1776 Massachusetts Ave. Washington, DC 20036	(202) 478-8500	www.thenational-campaign.org	Seeks to improve the well-being of children, youth and families by decreasing the rate of unwanted pregnancies through education and community involvement.
National Center on Elder Abuse	297 Graham hall Newark, DE 19716	(800) 677-1116	ncea.aoa.gov	Is committed to ensuring that older Americans will live with dignity. integrity, independence and without abuse, neglect and exploitation.
National Child Abuse Hotline	15757 N. 78th St. Suite B Scottsdale, AZ 85260	(800) 4ACHILD/ (800) 422-4453	www.childhelp. org	The confidential and anonymous hotline offers crisis intervention, information, literature and referrals to thousands of emergency, social service and support resources.
National Council on the Aging	1901 L St. NW Washington, DC 20036	(202) 479-1200	www.ncoa.org	Works with thousands of organizations across the county to help seniors live independently, find jobs and benefits, improve their health nd remain active in their communities.

National Domestic Violence Hotline	PO Box 161810 Austin, TX 78716	(800) 799-SAFE/ (800) 799-7233	www.ndvh.org	Provides crisis intervention, information and referral to victims of domestic violence, perpetrators, friends and families.
National Foundation for Credit Counseling	801 Roeder Rd. Suite 900 Silver Spring, MD 20910	(800) 388-2227	www.nfcc.org	Helps people get free or low-cost financial education and counseling services from trained, certified financial counselors
National Hospice Foundation	Department 6058 Washington, DC 20042	(800) 658-8898	www.hospiceinfo. org	Provides free resources and information to help people make decisions about end-of-life care and services before a crisis.
National Kidney Foundation	30 E. 33rd St. New York, NY 10016	(800) 622-9010	www.kidney.org	Is dedicated to preventing kidney disease, improving the health and well-being of individuals and families affected by kidney disease and increasing the availability of all organs for transplantation.
National Mental Health Association	2000 N. Beauregard St. Rockville, MD 20847	(800) 696-6642	www.nmha.org	Educates the general public about the realities of mental health and mental illness.
National Prevention Information Network	PO Box 6003 Rockville, MD 20849	(800) 458-5231	www.cdcnpin.org	A reference and referral service for information on HIV/AIDS, viral hepatitis, sexually transmitted diseases and tuberculosis.

C

F